Murray

November 1975

OUTCAST

ROSEMARY SUTCLIFF

OUTCAST

Illustrated by

RICHARD KENNEDY

London

OXFORD UNIVERSITY PRESS

Oxford University Press, Ely House, London W.1

GLASGOW NEW YORK TORONTO MELBOURNE WELLINGTON
CAPE TOWN IBADAN NAIROBI DAR ES SALAAM LUSAKA ADDIS ABABA
DELHI BOMBAY CALCUTTA MADRAS KARACHI LAHORE DACCA
KUALA LUMPUR SINGAPORE HONG KONG TOKYO

ISBN 0 19 271081 8

FIRST EDITION 1955
REPRINTED 1957, 1959, 1963, 1965, 1966, 1973

Printed in Great Britain by Fletcher & Son Ltd, Norwich

FOR MY FATHER

without whose help the *Alcestis* of the
Rhenus Fleet would never have been
seaworthy

———

*I should like also to thank Harold
Lawton, Indian Service of Engineers, for
his advice in draining Romney Marsh*

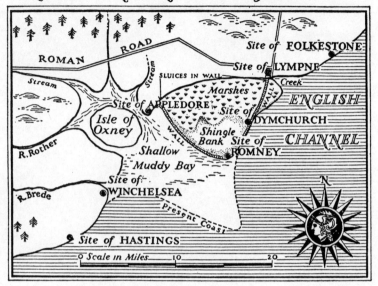

AUTHOR'S NOTE

Celt, Roman, Saxon, Norman and English have all had a hand in winning Romney Marsh from the sea, and making it safe afterwards. But it seems likely that it was the Romans with their genius for engineering who first began draining operations on a big scale. If that was so, then the Rhee Wall, the ancient sea defence which you can still trace here and there, running from Appledore to New Romney, may well have been built in the first place by just such a force of Legionaries working under just such an Engineer Centurion as I have made Beric find there when he comes to the Marsh, in the last part of this book.

CONTENTS

STORM ON THE COAST

THE gale, which had lulled for a little while, came swooping back with a shriek and a beating as of great wings against the village that crouched on the bare hill-shoulder, huddling close to the ground, as though for safety. In the house-place of Cunori, the Chieftain's brother, the hearth-smoke came billowing back in stinging clouds from the smoke-hole in the low turf roof, and the seal-oil lamp hanging from the roof-tree leapt and fluttered and sank, bringing the shadows crowding in, so that for a moment the storm and the things of the storm seemed to have broken through into the small round stronghold of warmth and safety that was Cunori's home. But the gust passed, as the others had done, and the lamp steadied, and the side-driven flames leapt up again on the hearth.

Cunori, sitting beside the fire, listened to the gale beating its wild wings all round the house-place, and was glad that the lambing was over and he need not go out again to-night. He leaned forward to catch the light on the spearhead to which he was fitting a new shaft. The old shaft, notched and splintered and warped from many hunts, lay beside him; and the new ashen shaft was satisfyingly white and straight as he fitted it into the socket; and the long, slender head caught the leaping firelight, so that it was like a tongue of flame between his hands. Three hounds lay a-sprawl on the rushes, with their bellies to the warmth: huge, brindled, wolf-seeming creatures. And on the far side of the fire—the Women's Side —Guinear sat spinning.

Cunori glanced at her from time to time as he worked, but she never raised her eyes from the whirling spindle with its growing spool of greyish wool. He wished that she would look up; he wished that she would stop spinning for a moment; he wished he could think of something to say that would make her laugh. He liked it when she laughed. That was one of the reasons why he had asked her of her father, two summers ago: so that he could have her laughter by his own fire. But she had not laughed for half a moon now—not since the babe died.

Cunori was sorry about the babe, though not so sorry as he would have been if it had been a son. Daughters could be set to help in the field-strips and so on, but almost as soon as they were large enough to be any use you had the trouble of getting them married, and once they were married, you might as well have never had daughters at all—better, indeed, because you had to give some of your own weapons to whoever it was who married them, to seal the bargain. Sons were quite another matter: they went with you on the hunting trail, and they brought their wives home to work on the family field-strips, and when you were too old to hunt, they hunted for you. When you had enough sons, it might be good to have daughters; a daughter before you had any sons at all was really something of a misfortune. But he knew that it did not seem like that to Guinear; all Guinear cared for was that it had been hers, and that it had lived only a day.

' If the harvest is good, I will give her a set of amber pins for her hair,' he thought, laying down the wolf-spear and taking up another that was in need of burnishing. 'And some cooking-pots; and if the harvest is *very* good, I will give her a length of fine striped cloth such as the merchants sell, to make a tunic.'

But he knew that the amber pins and the cooking-pots and even the fine striped cloth would not comfort Guinear for the loss of the babe; and that made him feel helpless, and feeling helpless was a thing that always made him angry; so he scowled at the spear-blade, rubbing harder and harder, as though he hated it.

The gale seemed to be rising higher than ever, and under the beating and howling of it a new note was swelling, now lost beneath the shriller overtones of the storm, now sounding clear: the deep, reverberating boom and crash that was the sea. The wind was going round to the north, piling the seas on to the black rocks of the headland, flinging in wave after wave like the blows of a hammer, as though to batter the cliffs to pulp.

He looked up with a start, and even Guinear checked her spinning, as a gust wilder than any that had gone before hurled itself upon the house-place with a drumming that shook the very roof-tree. Luath, the pack leader, opened eyes like twin yellow lamps in the wildly flickering gloom, and growled softly in his throat, then sprang up, followed by the rest, their hair rising along their necks, as the leather apron over the low, shielded entrance was plucked aside, and a figure came ducking in with the eddying gale behind it.

Cunori was afoot as swiftly as his hounds, grasping his hunting-spear in one hand while with the other he made the sign to avert evil. But the new-comer was neither live enemy nor storm-driven ghost, though from his appearance he might have been either; and as he came into the leaping flame-light, the great hounds ceased their sing-song snarling and lay down again, and Cunori tossed aside his spear. ' Flann! ' he cried disgustedly. ' You were never nearer to a spear between your ribs! What brings you abroad on such a night? '

Flann was gasping for breath as he stood before the entrance, shaking the wild hair out of his eyes. ' The red mare, in the first place,' he panted. ' She broke out again, and I have been right away over the sea-cliffs after her, and it was so that I saw it. There's a ship caught in the bay and trying to beat out round the headland. She will be on to the Killer Rock by now! '

Cunori's disgust was gone on the instant. He remembered the last time a ship had driven on to the Killer. There had been many things washed up by the sea afterwards. He said nothing, but his eyes met Flann's, and a fierce excitement leapt between them. Then, swinging round on the woman,

3

who had risen also, he demanded: 'My cloak! Quick! Bring me my cloak, Guinear.'

Flann had already disappeared again, to spread the news throughout the village, as she brought it to him. He caught it from her and flung it round his shoulders, stabbing home the bronze pin, and plunged out after Flann into the buffeting darkness, thrusting back the hounds who made to follow him. The wind almost took his breath away as he made his way down between the crowding huts to the gate of the stockade. Clearly he had not been the first to whom Flann had cried his news, for other dark figures were heading in the same direction, and when they reached it they found the thorn bush which normally blocked the gap at night had already been dragged aside by those who had gone before. They left it so, for those who came after them, and turned seaward, heads down and shoulders hunched, leaning into the wind.

The moon, which was near to full, seemed racing across the night, now lost behind great banks of tattered cloud now sailing out into ragged fjords of clear sky; and as it came and went, the tribesmen were now engulfed in bat-winged darkness, now flooded with swift silver radiance, as they struggled seaward.

The whole Men's Side of the village was out and heading for the coast and the promised wreck, streaming out hound-wise across the hills, eager for whatever harvest Camulus the Lord of Storms had sent their way. And among the rest, Cunori came at last over what seemed to be the edge of the world into the full onslaught of the shrieking gale and the salt taste of spindrift on his lips; and crouching against the thrust of the wind that strove to pluck him off and whirl him away like a blown leaf, looked down. From where he stood the cliff fell away in a gigantic tumble of turf-slopes and granite ledges, ending in the jagged thrust of rocks round which the water boiled in yeasty turmoil, whose farthest rock of all, lying hidden beneath the water save at low tide, was the Killer. And out on the Killer, caught and battered and already breaking up, was the ship that Flann had seen.

4

The moon, riding clear of the clouds at that moment, showed her clearly: a mastless, broken-backed thing that had once been a Roman merchantman. The watching tribesmen on the cliff-top had seen many such—transports and galleys, too—plying up and down to the great Legionary Station of Isca Silurium. Sometimes it happened, in a north-easterly wind, that a vessel would get embayed somewhere along the coast and be driven on to the rocks, and when that happened there were seldom any of the crew left to tell the tale; but afterwards their cargoes and their gear came ashore along with their drowned bodies.

Cunori held back the hair that whipped across his face, and gazed out towards the wreck, wondering how long she would hold together. Not long, he thought, not long in this sea; and he spared a moment to think that it would not be good to be in that ship now, before he plunged on down the narrow, swerving cliff-track to the sea.

Half-way down he all but fell over a squatting figure, and realized that it was Merddyn the Druid, Merddyn the old and crazy, who had once been powerful. The old man was crouching in the shelter of an outcropping rock, crooning to himself and swaying to and fro as he watched the scene below him. He looked up as Cunori halted an instant beside him, and laughed, with a high, inhuman, seabird note in his laughter. ' See there! ' he cried above the wind. ' See down there! A fine sight—a sight to warm the hands at as though it were a fire! Aiee! That was a great wave! Right over them! Another as great, and there will be one ship's crew the fewer of the Eagle People, to strut in the sun! One more wave. Oh, wave and king among waves, great white-maned, stallion-crested wave come swiftly and trample with your hooves and make an end, that the old heart of Merddyn the Druid may rejoice!'

Cunori left him and went on down the steep track, crouching against the wind. Below him the great waves thundered in, pounding upon the rocks, pounding upon the doomed ship; but indeed it was no ship now, only a pitiful broken thing that

5

grew smaller with every wave. On a level patch a little above the foot of the cliff the tribesmen were gathering. From here a man might almost have hurled a spear into the wreck; but the moon was dimming into the clouds again, and through the flung spray and turmoil of the storm they could see no sign of any life on board, nor hear any cry. There was nothing that the tribesmen could do to help, and even if there had been, they would scarcely have thought to try. To take from the sea was unlucky. If any man got ashore living, that was another matter; they would give him food and shelter, tend his hurts, and send him on his way. But from this wreck, in this sea, no man would get ashore living.

Rhythmically, remorselessly, the great waves came in, hurling against the rocks and breaking with a booming thunder that made the solid ground shudder under Cunori's feet. He was drenched with spray, dazed and stunned by the sheer stupendous tumult of wind and sea. The dimmed moon was brightening again, and by its light he saw, through the curtain of flying spume, the dark shape of the wreck; and even as he looked, a huge curled and crested wave reared up, arching over it: the great wave that Merddyn had called for. It broke with a crash that seemed to shake earth and sky, plunging and pouring down. Black reef and black wreck were engulfed in it, hidden in a boiling turmoil from which the spray burst upward in a spreading sheet and was whipped away by the wind. And when it cleared, the white water was sluicing down the crannies of the reef, boiling over the hidden Killer; and of the wreck there was no sign.

Even as the tribesmen watched, a great, silver-fringed cloud swept across the moon, and the world was quenched in darkness.

. . . . .

The gale, as though it had accomplished its purpose, began to abate from that moment, and it was in a spent grey dawn that the tribesmen went searching among the rocks along the Seal Strand a little back from the headland for the things that the storm had brought them.

6

A high grey sky, veined with blue and silver, arched above a gale-swept world, and the dying wind had gone round, so that in the lee of the cliffs it was almost still. But the great combers came rolling in in white unbroken ranks to crash and cream among the rocks and on the little shingle beaches. The tide was out, leaving the narrow beaches littered with the things that had come ashore already from the wreck: spars and timber and cordage that would all come in useful; a few carcasses of sheep; wineskins that came rolling in, and were gathered by men who made human chains and waded out to meet them; drowned seamen who must presently be given burial, lest their wet ghosts come dripping to the hearths of the village. With the next two tides there would be more, more of everything, all along the bay. No more after that.

Cunori, searching under the headland, with a mass of dripping cordage under one arm, was the first to find two bodies among the rocks. Most of those they had found so far had been seamen, but these were of a different kind. They were a man and a woman, held close in each other's arms with a clasp so strong that not even the rocks had been able to break it. They were both young. The man looked as though he were a soldier—a look which Cunori, himself a warrior, recognized: maybe a soldier going to join his Legion. The woman's long, wet hair, outflung across the rock, and trailing among the grey and olive sea-wrack, was golden brown. Lovely it must have been when it was dry, Cunori thought. He bent to look at the two more closely, and as he did so, something stirred between them.

With a startled exclamation, he drew back; then stooped closer, to investigate.

He found a wonder; one thing that had come alive out of that raging sea. Tightly lashed, with what looked like strips torn from a cloak, into the hollow of the man's shoulder, was a very young baby. It was the rocks, Cunori thought, rather than the sea, that had killed its mother and father, and their bodies had shielded the babe. Now it stirred, making a tiny, sick, crowing sound as it tried to breathe. It was blue, and half drowned: quite soon, if it were left to itself, it would be dead, too. And for a moment Cunori hesitated. It would be much less trouble to leave it there. Then, hardly knowing why, he took his hunting-knife from his belt and cut the strips of cloth that held it to its father, and lifted it clear. It was a man child, not more than four or five moons old, and it was quite unhurt. ' I must get the water out of this thing, or it will die,' Cunori thought, and he held it upside down and shook it. A little salt water came out of its mouth, and he went on shaking it. Suddenly it began to wail: a thin, bleating cry like that of a new-born lamb, but desperately weak. Cunori turned it right end up and looked at it in wonder, feeling the tiny life of it fluttering and fighting for existence between his hands; then with a hurried and almost shame-faced gesture bundled it into the folds of his wet cloak and stowed it in the crook of his arm against what little warmth there was in his own chilled body. Food, he thought; he must get it to food and warmth quickly, or that fighting spark of life in it would go out.

He cast one last uncertain look at the man and the woman. He did not think that they could have had any thought of saving the babe—not in such a sea and such a coast: they must have meant only that the three of them should be to-gether. But they *had* saved the babe; and Cunori wanted it. He wanted it for Guinear, because it might comfort her better than amber pins or a new cooking-pot could do. Holding it close against him, he turned to go.

He found himself face to face with Merddyn the Druid, and checked, startled. It was never pleasant to find Merddyn close to one unexpectedly; his eyes were yellow, cold and bright and hard as jewels in a face so gaunt that it was like a skull; uncomfortable eyes that went through a man and let in a cold wind behind them. Those eyes of his were fixed on Cunori now; he shook back the wild white hair that hung about his shoulders, and demanded: ' What thing is that you have under your cloak, Cunori, son of Cuthlyn? '

' It is a man child, and it lives, Old Father,' said

Cunori, perfectly aware that Merddyn knew that as well as he did.

' And what do you do with the man child? '

' I take it to my woman, in place of her own that died half a moon since.'

' It is unlucky to rob the sea,' Merddyn said, licking his lips. ' If you bring it among us, it will bring sorrow on us all—sorrow and to spare on those who rob the sea.'

' The sea does not want him,' Cunori returned stubbornly, instantly stiffening in his determination to have the thing, at the first hint of opposition—just as the first thing that had made him determined to have Guinear had been the discovery that a hunter called Istoreth wanted her. ' The sea has refused him and cast him out. He was not born to be drowned, this one.'

' Nonetheless, evil will come of it, evil and the wrath of the Gods, if you bring the thing among us! It is a Roman whelp, and what have we to do with such—we, the Free People beyond the frontier? It is of the breed that tore apart the Holy Places and slaughtered my brethren, sixty winters ago, and reft from us the power that was ours—ours to us, who were the holders of the secrets of life, the moon-crested, before their coming! ' The old man's voice had risen to its seabird note, and drawn by it, tribesmen were gathering from all directions, scrambling towards them over the rocks to discover the reason for the outcry.

Cunori was exasperated. Quite suddenly he wondered how it was, if the Druids had indeed been the masters of all power, as Merddyn claimed, that they had allowed themselves to be overcome by the Eagle People. He flung the thought away from him in a scared hurry, furtively spreading the fingers of his left hand to avert evil. But all the same, he was going to have the babe. ' Old Father,' he said, ' I will give you a black ram lamb for the gods, so that they may not be angry.'

And he stepped past the old man, his fingers still spread hornwise, and set off along the shore towards the cliff path.

Some of his Spear Brethren crowded in on him as he went, and he cried out to them, half laughing, half angry: 'Off! Get off! I must get this thing home to my woman, or it will die.' And he strode past them, leaving them to stare after him, leaving Merddyn the Druid muttering and mouthing in their midst, torn by the cruel awareness that sixty winters ago no man would have dared to withstand his will, nor sought to buy the Gods with a black ram lamb; and the young soldier and his wife lying with their arms round each other on the wet rocks.

Istoreth—that same Istoreth who had wanted Guinear—cried out a charm against ill luck, and spat towards Cunori as he passed him. Cunori laughed and spat back, then turned to the cliff path. He reached the cliff-top, and set off at a swift wolf-lope for the village. His dogs came out to meet him as he drew near to his own house-place, whining and thrusting round him; and he ordered them off much as he had done his Spear Brothers. 'Off, Luath. Off, Keri! Back, I say!' He ducked under the low lintel and plunged down into the warm gloom of the house-place.

Guinear was stirring the morning stew, and she sat back on her heels, still holding the pottery spoon, and looked up at him, questioningly. 'How went the hunting?'

'Well enough,' Cunori said.

'Did many things come ashore?'

'Wineskins and timber, and a few carcasses of sheep, on this tide.'

'And—drowned men? No one saved?'

Cunori hesitated, and as he did so the babe under his cloak gave a little sick whimper. Guinear started as though she had been struck. She put both hands to her mouth, and pressed them there, staring at him with widened eyes. 'What have you under your cloak?' she asked after a moment, in a harsh whisper.

Cunori squatted down beside her, almost in the warm ash of the fire, and put back the wet folds. 'See,' he said; 'I brought it for you. Take it.'

But she made no move to take it. 'No!' she whispered. 'Oh no, no!'

'It is a fine little cub,' Cunori persisted, thrusting away with his free hand an exploring grey muzzle that came under his arm.

'It is not mine,' she said flatly.

'If you do not take it soon it will not matter whose it is,' Cunori said. 'And I might as well have left it on the rocks below the headland where I found it, to die with its mother.'

She raised her eyes swiftly to his face. 'Its mother?'

Cunori told her how he had found the babe, and she listened, looking from him to the tiny spent thing in his hands and back. But she only said again: 'It is not mine; not my babe.'

'Nevertheless, do you take it. It is a fine cub, a man cub!' Cunori poked the baby at her, hopefully, but she flinched away. The warmth had begun to revive the faint life that still flickered in the creature, and suddenly it set up a thin, exhausted crying. Cunori looked anxiously at Guinear; he had been so set on bringing her the babe—it had seemed as though it was meant for her; he had not thought about it very clearly, but he felt very clearly indeed that she had lost a child and it had lost its mother, and somehow it was right that they should be put together. It fitted, and he liked things to fit.

But the terribly thin wailing did what all Cunori's urging could not do. Quite suddenly, with a little sound that was almost a sob, Guinear leaned forward and reached out her hands. 'Give him to me,' she said. 'It is not so that you should hold a babe.'

PACK LAW

THEY called him Beric, and Cunori gave a black ram lamb to the gods for him; and he had his first taste of solid food from the tip of Cunori's dagger so that he might grow up to be a great warrior. And in his second year Guinear pricked the warrior patterns of the tribe on his brown baby skin, and rubbed woad into the prick-marks, and afterwards gave him as much wild honeycomb as ever he could eat, to comfort the smart of his wounds and still his howling.

Nine times the gales of autumn beat over the village; nine times the lambing season came round and the Men's Side kept the wolf guard on the sheep-folds through the bitter winter nights; nine times the sea-pinks bloomed along the cliffs, spilling down to join hands with the spray that beat upon the rocks below. And there were three sons in Cunori's houseplace; and it was time for Beric, the eldest of them, to begin his training.

Every year when the harvest was in there came a great day in the village, and from all the Clan territory the people poured into it. They gathered in the open space at the heart of the village, where the cattle were penned in time of trouble; and there, in the presence of the whole Clan, all the boys who had turned fifteen since last harvest received their weapons from their fathers, and became men and warriors. And after that the cooking-pits were opened and the whole roast boar carcasses lifted out, and there was a great feast, with much heather beer and harp music; and the warriors of the Clan danced the Dance of Fire and the Dance of the Chariot Charge and the Dance of New Spears, under the admiring eyes of the Women's Side. Before the Romans came with their meddlesome patrols it had been a much greater day, and

13

all the Clans of the Dumnonii had gathered together at the Tribal Dun at Uxella, and there had been long and terrible rites that were secret between the Druids and the New Spears, before the boys received their weapons. The glory was departed now, before the shadow of the Eagles, and the great and powerful Druid-kind had almost ceased to be. Beric could just remember the Druid of his own Clan; yellow eyes, he had had, that went right through you and let in a cold wind behind them. But he was dead long ago, and now the Clan had no one to officiate at the Rites any more. But it was still a great day, and between the roast boar and the warrior-dancing the boys who had turned nine since last harvest, and so were due to begin their training, were thrust into the firelit Council circle, to be looked over and approved by the Clan.

Beric, sitting cross-legged among Cunori's hounds, and watching the new warriors one by one salute the setting sun with upraised spear, thought of the time when he would have finished his training: when he would stand where the New Spears stood now, and turn toward the setting sun and bring his spear crashing down across his new shield, and take his place for the first time among the warriors of the Clan. Then he would ride with his Spear Brothers on the war trail, and have a voice at the Council Fire, and the right to wear the warrior scarlet. That would be good.

He came out of a proud and happy dream that had lasted him through a large meal of sizzling boar-flesh eaten off the point of his dagger, to find that dusk had turned to dark, and the Chieftain had raised his voice from beside the Council Fire, and was calling for the nine-year-olds. Beric hastily thrust his dagger back into his belt, wiped off some of the boar's grease on to the nearest hound, and went to answer the summons. From all over the open space the nine-year-olds were gathering, five from the village, twice as many more from the outlying Clan, scrambling over outstretched legs and picking their way between the many hounds, to arrive at last in the firelit circle under the critical gaze of the chief hunters and warriors of the Clan. There they stood, staring

14

straight before them or grinning uncertainly at their fathers and each other, and not quite sure what to do with their arms and legs, while the elders of the Clan looked them over.

Cunori sat close to the Chieftain by right of kinship. He looked up as Beric entered the ring, and gave him a quick nod of encouragement, which sent a warm wave of pride through him. Beric knew how he had come into Cunori's household, but he knew it only as a story, not as anything that really touched him. In his world, the only world he knew, Cunori was his father and Guinear his mother, and Arthmail and Arthgal his brothers. And just now his one thought was to make a good showing before the Clan so that his father might be proud of the eldest son of his house.

The elders of the Clan were looking them over carefully, nodding to each other. 'A likely lot,' they said, 'a good lot this year, a very good lot, on the whole. But that one—that one,' and Beric found that they were looking at him, eyes all round the circle looking at him, doubtfully. Then the big red-haired Chieftain with the gold torc round his neck beckoned him closer; and Beric went with very stiff legs and stood in front of him, suddenly afraid.

'What shall we do with this one, my brothers?' said the Chieftain. 'This foster son of the house of Cunori? It is time that we chose the trail for him. Nine years he has lived among us, but he is not one of us, and shall we then take him into the Spear Brotherhood of the Clan?'

Cunori spoke up hotly from his place near the Chieftain. 'He is one of us in all things but that he was not born of our blood.'

'It is a large "but",' said another man, leaning forward into the firelight.

Cunori rounded on him. 'Is it a larger "but" than beats in your own veins, Istoreth? You who claim descent from the Seal Folk, the People of the Sea? Was not that Seal forefather of yours accepted into the Spear Brotherhood?'

'The Seal People are of our world,' said Istoreth fiercely. 'The Red Crests are not, and this fosterling of yours carries

15

his breed in his face. I have been eastward across the frontier to sell pelts, and I have seen them, the Red Crests, and I know. Flann, Gourchien, you also, you have seen them often; look at him. How shall he run with our sons and carry his spear among us hereafter?'

There was a low, growling murmur from the men round the fire; Cunori, his hand leaping to his dagger, had begun a furious retort, and for a moment it looked as if there might be trouble—the kind of snapping, snarling trouble that breaks out suddenly between hounds—for all men knew how little love was lost between Cunori and Istoreth.

Then the Chieftain cut in: 'Better send him across the frontier to his own kind.'

'And what shall he do across the frontier with his own kind?' Cunori demanded furiously. 'We are all the kind he knows, and he is but nine summers old.'

'There are tradesmen enough at Isca Dumnoniorum who will take him in to learn a trade,' said the Chieftain, kindly enough.

But before anyone could reply, Beric himself took up the fight.

All this while he had stood very still, staring at each speaker in turn, while the roast boar meat turned cold and heavy in his stomach. Now he drew himself up and faced the Chieftain like a small wild thing at bay. 'What have I to do with the Red Crests, that I should go to them now? You are my people, my own people, by hearth-fire and bread and salt, and I will not go to Isca Dumnoniorum and learn a trade; I will learn to be a hunter and a warrior with the rest of my kind.' His voice cracked a little, but he managed to steady it, as he swung round on the circle of the warriors. 'Oh, elders of my Clan, I have not done anything *wrong*, that you should cast me out!'

There was a long silence, and then out of the circle two spoke up for Beric.

The first of them was Rhiada, the blind harper, who sat on a deerskin at the Chieftain's feet; and he drew a hand across

16

his harp-strings, so that the firelight played on them as on running water and the harp-notes sprang up towards the stars like a bird released; and he flung back his head and laughed up at Beric. 'So, that was boldly spoken for a nine-year-old. I do not see his people in his face, but I know a bold heart when I meet one. What matter where the blood comes from, so that it runs hot and true, my brothers?'

And the second was Ffion, who, before he grew old and white-haired, had been the greatest hunter in the Clan; and he leaned forward into the firelight and said in his old gentle voice: 'Let him run with the pack. If he can hold his own with them after this night's work, he will make a warrior worth having. He comes of a warrior people, though not ours. . . . I have reared a wolf-cub before now; he was not a dog, but he hunted with me as a dog, none better.'

For a while the argument raged, for Istoreth was not one to give in easily, and he had a certain following among the younger hunters. But Ffion had been a great man in the Clan almost as long as the oldest of them could remember, and the word of a harper was not a thing to be lightly set aside. Also, being all of them warriors, the game-cock way in which the boy had spoken up for himself appealed to them. And so at last, looking round the firelit circle, the Chieftain said: 'So be it, then; let him start his training with the rest, and may he make a warrior indeed.'

'And may he not bring sorrow and to spare upon the Clan, even as Merddyn foretold!' said Istoreth savagely, and turned his attention back to his mead horn.

'As to that, there was the matter of a black ram lamb,' said Ffion quellingly.

And Beric, his future settled on the word of Rhiada and Ffion, found himself with his fellows, who had been open-mouthed onlookers all this while, thrust out of the firelit circle.

The whole scene was breaking up and shifting, as people began to press back against the huts, leaving the open space clear in the moonlight for dancing. Beric did not stay with the other boys, but slipped away among the crowd. And when he glimpsed his mother carrying a mead jar on her hip, he dodged away before she saw him, for he knew that she would have seen and heard all that had happened, and he was desperately afraid that if she caught him she might try to comfort him, and he could not have borne to be comforted, just then. He took the hurt away with him as though it were a sore that he was afraid of anyone touching, and found Bran, the wisest of all his father's hounds, and squatted down beside him in a dark corner between two huts. He put his arms round the dog's warm neck, and Bran licked his face from ear to ear.

There in the dark corner they remained for a long time, while out on the moon-silvered, fire-gilded space before them the Men's Side kept up the stamping whirl and the rhythmic shouting of the warrior dances; and the weapons clashed and the sparks flew up from the swirling torches.

All was well now—of course it was. He was going to train with the other boys, and wear the warrior scarlet by and by. These were his people, his own people. But it was the first time that he had ever told himself so, for it was the first time that he had ever needed to. The glory was gone from the night; and the heavy coldness was still in his stomach where there should have been only a pleasant sensation of much boar meat.

But by next morning he had almost forgotten the coldness in his stomach. That day the people from the outlying villages started home, and there was a great turmoil of barking dogs, restive ponies, and missing babies that went on almost all day. And on the morning after that, when he woke in the living-hut where he slept with his father and mother and two small brothers and many dogs, he remembered only that it was the day on which he was to begin his warrior training.

His mother gave him an extra lump of wild honeycomb with his barley cake and milk that morning; and Arthmail, who was six, and Arthgal, who was only four, watched him with round, worshipful eyes while he ate it; and his father let him

18

choose one for himself from among his light throwing-spears. And Beric tightened the strap of deerskin round his middle that kept up his kilt, and took his chosen javelin, and set out.

Down between the huts he trotted: stone-built huts, squatting low under their turf roofs, with nothing to tell which was house-place and which stable or byre or store-shed, save the blue woodsmoke that rose like so many jays' feathers from the roofs of the living-huts into the morning air as he trotted by. He went out through the gateway in the high, thorn-crested bank, and down into the upland valley where the little field-strips clung for shelter to the lee slopes of the land. Here, on the edge of the forest of wind-stunted oak and thorn that swept up like a dark sea from farther inland, was a strip of rough grass running down to the stream, which had been the training ground for the village ever since there had been a village at all. Here the practice posts were set up for Charioteers in the making, and for twenty years and more old Pridfirth had taught the first handling of spear and javelin to the boys of the village.

Several boys were there already when Beric arrived, tumbling over each other like puppies, while Pridfirth sat on a fallen tree-trunk and ignored them; and the rest came hard on his heels to the training ground. There were only a hand-ful of them, and none were very old, for after about their second year the boys passed out of Pridfirth's hands into the hands of hunters who were younger and had not so many wolf-bites to make them stiff.

It was Pridfirth's custom, after trying them out, to tell the new-comers that they were not what their fathers had been. And this morning he followed his custom, first making each of them in turn throw their javelins at a rough straw target, and then telling them what he thought of them, more in sorrow than in anger, sitting on his tree-trunk while they stood before him; and the boys who had been through it last year gathered joyfully to listen. 'Your fathers were not much to crow about,' he said, 'but they did at least know what a javelin was *for*. Now you!' and he continued to tell them

19

about themselves in detail, until they turned pink and scuffled. ' But since something must be made of you, lest the Clan lack hunters hereafter,' he finished wearily, ' we will now begin.'

And begin they did. There were four new straw targets— one daubed with red stain, one with black, one with green, and one left the natural gold of the straw—and the older boys threw their javelins at these, Pridfirth crying out the colour so that they never knew until the last instant which of the four they were to aim at. But the new-comers had only one target, and that first day they seldom got as far as aiming even at that, for they were learning how to stand, how to swing forward, at what instant to send the javelin free so that swing and throw were one perfect curve of movement. They had all handled their father's weapons since they could stagger, but they had had no particular training, save what they had picked up in imitation of their elders, and some of them were slower than others to get the feel of what they were trying to do. But Pridfirth was very patient with them, showing them over and over again. . . . ' Set this foot farther out; now— over and forward. That was better; now again. No, *no*, child, do not jerk the thing away as though it were a hornet; smoothly—smoo-oothly, I said. . . . It is not enough to stand like a tree-stump and throw with one arm; you are one curve, you and your javelin, springing right from your big toe to the tip of the blade. Try again.'

And Beric watched and listened and obeyed, working as he had never worked before; so that by the end of the lesson he was really beginning to have some idea of what it was all about. And then he was happy.

But after the lesson was over and Pridfirth had gone about his own affairs, with the appalling swiftness of a nightmare in which familiar things suddenly become strange and horrible, Beric's whole familiar world turned traitor.

It began when he looked up from slackening the strap round his middle, to see several of the boys crowding in on him with jeering, hostile faces.

' Beric has been working very hard,' said one.

20

'He need not waste his sweat. Everyone knows the Red Crests are as much use as cows on the hunting trail!' said another.

'Red Crest!' chanted a third; and they began to jostle him. 'Ya-ee! Red Crest! Why don't you go back to your own people?'

Beric faced them, panting a little. All his life he had played and fought and tumbled about with these boys, his pack-brothers; and neither he nor they had had any thought of his not being one of them. But that was all over, since two nights ago. He knew now what old Ffion had meant when he said: 'If he can hold his own with the pack, after this night's work, he will make a warrior worth the having.' He understood perfectly what was happening. He had seen the hound-pack turn on a strange dog before now, or one that was hurt, or different from themselves in any way.

A second-year boy, Cathlan by name, came thrusting through the rest, and gave him a casual buffet on the side of the head. 'We don't want little strutting Red Crests in the Spear Brotherhood,' he said.

Beric staggered, for the blow had been a heavy one; then, with his ear ringing, he recovered himself. 'Don't you? But you are going to get one!' he shouted, and hit Cathlan full on the mouth with all the strength that was in him.

There was a long-drawn gasp from the rest, and Beric, watching the surprise and rage on Cathlan's face, expected the whole lot of them on top of him next breath, pulling him down like hounds on their quarry. But the rush did not come, and vaguely, as Cathlan flung himself upon him, he realized that the others had drawn back a little, leaving an open space around the two of them. It was to be single combat, then, the stranger against the chosen champion of the pack.

Cathlan was a year older than Beric, and more than a year heavier; also he was a renowned fighter, whereas Beric had never fought in earnest before. But he was fighting in earnest now, fighting for his place in the Clan, and he knew it. He fought like a wild cat, hitting out savagely again and again,

21

with no thought to guard against the hurly-burly blows that he got in return. All around them the squealing and yelping uproar rose, shriller and shriller yet, as the excitement of the onlookers mounted; but in the midst of it he and Cathlan fought in panting silence. They were down on the ground now, rolling over and over in a mass of flailing arms and legs, hitting wildly at each other with short jabbing blows. Then, quite how it happened Beric never knew, Cathlan was underneath. His freckled face all battered and smeared, he glared up at Beric; his mouth was shut tight, and he breathed through flaring nostrils like a stallion, as he struggled to get uppermost. Beric clung on, sobbing, and very near to his last gasp; blood from his nose was spattering down on to the other boy's furious upturned face; he felt sick and his heart seemed bursting. He set his teeth, and with one last effort, gripping his squirming enemy between his knees, he got Cathlan's ears in his hands and banged his head again and again on the hard-beaten ground.

He saw the fury turn vague and stupid in the other boy's face, and felt the fight go out of him. He gave Cathlan's head a final bang; then he staggered to his feet, and stood with the back of one hand pressed against his dripping nose, staring down at his fallen enemy. Cathlan lay where he was for the space of a dozen heart-beats, and then got up more slowly, licking a burst lip. For a long moment the two stood looking at each other, breathing hard. Then Beric turned on his heel, and with his bleeding nose in the air walked away. The little silent crowd parted, with a new respect, to let him through.

Looking neither to right nor left, he walked straight up through the oak woods, and over the bare hill-shoulder beyond, where the brood mares were at run with their feather-tailed foals beside them; on and on until he came out on to the headland, and along it to its farthermost end. And there, where two paces more would carry him into the Western Sea, he flung himself down on the coarse grass of the cliff-top.

Ever since he had been strong enough on his legs to get down the steep cliff-tracks, the shelving rocks of the Seal

Strand had been a favourite haunt of his; but he seldom came right out here to the Point, because he knew that it was among the rocks of the Point that Cunori his father had found him after the great storm, and the place made him feel unsafe, as though it were a weak spot in the circle of his familiar world, through which another world might break in on him. But to-day the very feeling that usually kept him away from the Point drew him out to it. It was all very odd and bewildering.

There was an ache in his stomach that was not hunger; an ache that was quite different from anything he had known before, and which he did not understand. He would be free to run with the pack now, he knew that: and yet he felt all the desolation of an outcast. He had won his first fight, and he was triumphant with a hard, harsh triumph. He was afraid, because he had come face to face with things that he had never dreamed of, and the sure foundations of his world had shifted under his feet. He was angry with almost everything under the sun, without quite knowing why; he was lost and shaken and bewildered, and his bruises hurt, and it was all these things twisted together into a hard knot within him that made the ache in his stomach.

'There is a great stone in my belly,' he told the wheeling gulls, ' and I do not understand, I do not understand.'

He noticed the dried blood on the back of his hand, and licked it off, tasting it salt, with a sweetness under the salt. He lay for a long time on his front, looking down. There was a lazy wind blowing, stirring the dry heads of the sea-pinks on the ledges, and sighing through the rough grass by his ear, with a clear, high note—almost a singing—above the soft, wet roar of the never-ceasing surge. The sea was lazy too, the slow, unceasing combers breaking far out, the foam-laced shallows playing delicately, kitten-wise, with the black rocks and the little shingle beaches. He watched the water come swinging in, greening as it shallowed, laced and curdled and frilled with foam, with a slap and a delicate curl-back on to itself as it met the flat surface of a rock, creaming up between them in threads of white; then draining out again with a

shrill hushing over the shingle, to join with the next wave—
and the next—and the next. Sometimes a gull's wings would
sweep by below him; once it was the grey-blue wings of a
peregrine falcon who had an eyrie on one of the ledges with
two young in it. But he did not watch them. The stone in
his belly came between him and them, and he had too many
things to think about.

His own father and mother, for instance. He had scarcely
ever thought about his own father before, because Cunori had
always been there, filling that place for him; and he had
never thought about his own mother at all, because it was beyond him to imagine any mother but Guinear. But he
thought about them now, watching the lazy wavelets creaming
among those black rocks, realizing suddenly, and for the first
time, that they had not been just people in a story, but real
people, though he knew nothing about them save that his
father had looked like a soldier, and his mother had had
golden-brown hair. His people, and he theirs.

A slight movement close to him made him look round; and
there, just squatting on to his haunches a few paces away, was
Cathlan.

Beric rolled over and sat up, ready for the fight to begin
again if it had to; and the two of them sat and looked at each
other. Cathlan's face was smeared with dried blood, and his
bruises were dark upon him; but he did not look as though he
had come to re-start the fight; and there was an odd expression on his battered face—a sort of elaborate carelessness.

'What have you come here for?' Beric demanded in a small,
gruff voice.

'It is hot,' said Cathlan, 'and I am very bloody. I came
to bathe.'

'There is water in the stream by the training ground.'

'Too crowded,' said Cathlan, with a sniff. 'All the rest
are splashing in it; besides, I like best to bathe in the
sea.'

'Go you and bathe in the sea, then,' said Beric.

'Umph!' grunted Cathlan non-committally. He stared

thoughtfully at a gull that swept overhead. 'Let you and me go down to the Seal Strand and bathe now,' he suggested.

'I do not want to bathe.'

'Come on,' Cathlan urged, still casually. 'You are all bloody too, and your nose wants washing.'

'Your mouth looks like a blackberry,' Beric told him.

Cathlan began to grin and checked as he discovered that it hurt. 'I know. It was a good fight.'

There was another silence, but of quite a different kind. 'Yes,' Beric said at last, wonderingly. 'Yes.'

'I'll wager there would not be two better fighters than you and me in all the Dumnoni,' said Cathlan, with deep satisfaction. 'Let you and me go and bathe now.'

They got to their feet, and made their way back along the headland, pulling off their kilts as they ran, scrambling down to the shelving rocks where the grey seals came to bask at ebb tide. And there, sitting in the swinging, foam-laced shallows, they washed each other's hurts with great thoroughness.

From that day forward, Beric and Cathlan hunted together.

III
THE OUTCAST

So for six years Beric ran with the pack, learning to be a warrior and a hunter; something of a farmer too, though the cattle and the field-strips were for the most part tended by the women. He learned to handle horse and hound, sword and spear and the man-high long-bow of the tribes. He learned to follow a three-day-old spoor as though it were a beaten trail. And little by little he forgot, almost as completely as the rest of the pack seemed to do, that he had ever had to fight for his right to run with them.

When he was twelve, Keri, the beautiful, brindled mate of Bran, had puppies; and Cunori gave the finest of the litter to Beric, to be his own hunting companion. Beric called the pup Gelert, and for long months, during which he learned as much as Gelert did, he gave up every free moment to training him; so that by the time the hound was a year old and the boy thirteen, they could think with one mind, as a hunter and his hound should do.

And then at last the fifteenth harvest of his life was gathered in, and the Feast of New Spears came round again, and it was time for Beric to receive his weapons and become a man. At fifteen, he was smaller and stockier than his fellows, with narrower hands and feet, but despite Istoreth's accusation of six years ago, there was little in his square brown face with the cleft chin and level eyes, nor in his tawny colouring, to set him apart from the rest. Many races went to the making of Rome, and if there was Latin blood in him, without doubt there was Celtic also. Certainly, standing with the other boys of his year on this long-awaited Night of New Spears, he had no thought of any difference between them. His mind did go back to that other Feast of New Spears, six years ago, to the

26

small boy who had looked forward so eagerly to this one—
and to what had happened after; but only as one looks back
to old, unhappy things that have nothing to do with the
present. The present was good, and the future would be good
too, the future in which he and Cathlan together would become great men in their Clan, hunters and warriors without
equal.

But the future which looked to Beric that night to be as
straight and shining as the white ash shaft of his new war-
spear, was to be a very different one, after all.

The months that followed his initiation into the Men's Side
were bad months for the Clan; bad ones for the whole tribe.
The harvest had been a lean one, wrecked by summer storms,
and all through the autumn and the wild wet winter the
hunting was bad; and when the lambing time came many of
the lambs were born dead, and often the ewes died too, as
happened sometimes in a wet season. Just after the turn of
the year one of the Clan's chief hunters was killed by a boar.
Spring came suddenly and early, but instead of better times, it
brought fever.

It was after the fever came that Beric began to notice people
looking at him; looking and whispering. At first he thought
that he was imagining things, or maybe sickening for the
pestilence himself, but soon he realized that it was not that.
The Men's Side began to leave a little space between him and
them when they gathered together. Only Cunori his father
and Rhiada the Harper seemed untouched by the general
unease; and Cathlan, who stood shoulder to shoulder with
him on all occasions, with a bright-eyed defiance that somehow hurt Beric more deeply than the drawing aside of the
other men could do. Once he saw a woman make the sign
against evil as she passed him. He did not need to wonder
what it all meant, for deep within him, he knew; and the
knowledge turned him cold, remembering that six-year-
distant fight with Cathlan, and the hostile faces of the other
boys crowding in on him; remembering the dog-pack turning
on the stranger in their midst. But with the surface of his

mind he could not believe that such a thing could happen—not to him—not at the hands of his brothers.

It was Merddyn who had sown the seeds of the mischief; Merddyn the Druid, dead these many years. Merddyn had foretold the wrath of the Gods on the Clan for taking into itself one of the accursed breed that had torn apart their holy places and butchered their priesthood. People had not paid much heed at the time, for the old man was crazy; they had forgotten, when he died, and only remembered a little, six harvests ago. But now they were beginning to remember very clearly, the memory running to and fro among them like a rising wind through long grass. They looked at each other, and saw the memory behind each other's eyes, and Istoreth, who had not forgotten his grudge against Cunori, whistled it up again if ever it looked like sinking so that it grew and gained strength.

On an evening towards the end of the spring, Beric came home late to the evening meal which he knew his mother would be keeping warm for him, and found her alone in the big living-hut, and sitting idle with her hands in her lap, which was a thing very strange with her. She looked up quickly as he entered, and at sight of her white, strained face he checked on the threshold, while Gelert brushed past him and padded over to the fire.

' Mother, what is wrong? ' he asked in swift anxiety. ' Where are Father and the small ones? '

' I have sent Arthmail and Arthgal to my sister's for a little,' she said dully. ' Your father is with the rest of the Men's Side round the Council Fire. Did you not see the gathering as you came by? '

He shook his head. ' I have been up along the hill-run, trying out the black colt, and I came in by the higher gateway. I'll go down——'

' No! ' his mother cried; and then added more quietly: ' Eat your supper first. It has been keeping warm a long time, and see, it is your favourite—venison stew with herbs.' She took a smoking bowl from the hot ash as she spoke, thrusting aside Gelert's enquiring muzzle.

Beric never moved from the threshold. Suddenly his throat felt dry. ' This gathering—has it to do with me? '

His mother hesitated, looking into the bowl of stew, and then up into his eyes. Still carrying the bowl, though she had clearly forgotten about it with most of her mind, she rose, and came to him in the entrance. ' It has to do with you.'

' I will go down and take my place in it,' Beric said.

' No. You must bide until you are summoned.'

He went past her and sat down miserably beside the fire. ' They think it is through me that the lambing was bad this year and the pestilence has come,' he said. ' I know.'

His mother followed him, still with the bowl. ' Beric, Little Cub, try to eat. You must be hungry.'

He took the bowl from her and tried, but he was not hungry now, though he had been very hungry a few moments ago. He was still trying when a shadow darkened the entrance, and Cunori entered.

Beric sprang to his feet, oversetting the bowl, and stood looking at him with in-caught breath; then realized sickeningly that Cunori was finding it hard to meet his eyes. The silence hung heavy between them. ' I am to go down with you, to the Council Fire? ' he asked at last.

The other nodded, watching the hounds as they brushed past him to snuffle into the rushes after the spilled stew. Then he raised his head and looked at Beric: an odd look, troubled, angry, and ashamed. ' Bring your weapons with you, my son.'

Without a word, Beric turned to the far shadows, and took from their usual place his heron-tufted war-spear and proud bronze shield. He felt quite numb, as one can feel from a blow, if it be hard enough. Part of him had known that this was coming, but he had contrived somehow to hide the knowledge from himself because the thing had been too horrible to look at. And now it had come.

Still without a word, without even a glance at his mother standing as though frozen beside the hearth, he turned to follow his father out into the dusk. In the doorway he checked an instant to thrust back Gelert, who tried to follow him; then he went on.

Spear in hand, shield high on shoulder, he strode down towards the glow of the fire that he could see between the crowding huts. The whole village seemed gathered in the central space, when he came out into it; the Men's Side gathered with their hounds around the Council Fire, and behind them, out of the direct range of the firelight, a dim crowd in the dusk that he knew were the women and boys. In the utter silence they parted to let him through, and, obeying a gesture from his father, he passed him, and walked forward, down the broad, hostile lane that opened for him, out into the firelit circle; and came to a stand, just as he had done six harvests ago, before the place where the Chieftain sat.

He had seen this happen once before, when a hunter had broken the laws of the Tribe—the accused man standing with his weapons, here before the Chieftain's place, for the judgement of his spear brothers. If the judgement was for him, he would leave the Council Fire carrying his weapons as he had come; if he were to die or be driven out, he would leave his weapons to lie beside the Council Fire, since he had lost the right to them.

' I have brought Beric, my foster son, even at the bidding of the Council,' said Cunori's voice behind him.

The Chieftain looked up, fondling the head of a favourite hound as it rested on his thigh. ' Does Beric, your foster son, know why he comes here? '

' Aye, he knows.'

' Then there is little more that need be said.' The Chieftain glanced round the circle of firelit faces. ' Look well upon this Beric of the household of Cunori; look well, my brothers, and say, once and for all—what is your judgement? '

' Aye, look well! ' It was Istoreth, leaning forward into the firelight and pointing at him, half jeering, half in bitter earnest. ' Look at him, standing in your midst, people of the Dumnoni! Look at him, Cunori son of Cuthlyn, you who brought him among us to bring ruin on us all! What did

Merddyn the Druid foretell in the day that you took him from
the sea? Woe and wailing and the wrath of the Gods upon
the Clan—upon the whole Tribe—if ye brought into it a
whelp of the Red Crests. Merddyn warned ye, all of ye, but
ye would not listen; and see what has come of it! Lean
harvests and dead ewes, bad hunting and pestilence!' He
looked round at the rest, his lips drawn back in a snarl,
his dark eyes glittering in the firelight. ' Now, before it is too
late, before yet greater evils fall upon the Clan, we must drive
him out! Drive him out, I say, that he may take the anger of
the Gods with him, and the good times may return!'

All round the fire there rose a fierce muttering of agreement; and behind him, Beric heard Cunori's voice raised in
furious protest. ' Amgerit the Chieftain, you who are also
my brother, is there no justice left in the Clan? Beric my
foster son has done no wrong; he has kept the laws of the
Tribe, and there is no fault in him that you should drive him
out!'

' All this you have said before, and many times, Cunori my
brother.' The Chieftain's mouth was grim under the
drooping red wings of his moustache. ' All this we know well
enough. It is for no wrong that he has done that we drive
him out, but for what he is—for the blood that beats in him
which is not our blood and which has brought down on us the
wrath of our Gods. That also has been said many times.'

Yes, it had all been said, Beric thought drearily, in the
brief hush that followed—everything that there was to say,
over and over again. It was finished; and they were going to
drive him out. He looked round at the crowding circle of
warriors, their fierce faces set against him in the leaping flame-
light; looked round at them with a kind of numbed horror.
He had known no other life than life among these men.
They were his world, as surely as though he had indeed been
born to Guinear his mother in the house-place up yonder.
They were his kin in all but blood; the young men who had
hunted with him, the old ones who had taught him all he
knew. And now they were casting him out, and for no fault

32

—for mercifully it never occurred to him to wonder if he had indeed brought the anger of the Gods upon them.

But the firelight showed him two faces that differed from the rest: Cathlan's face, the eyes in it wide and bright and hot, and the face of Rhiada the Harper, sitting on his deerskin at the Chieftain's feet; and Rhiada's mouth looked wry, as though he had bitten a sloe. As you looked into other men's eyes to know what they were thinking, so you could tell what Rhiada was thinking by looking at his mouth. They had been fighting for him, those two; but what could they say? 'He has not broken the laws of the Tribe,' Rhiada might have said, as Cunori his father had done; and Cathlan might have said, 'He is my friend, and he saved me from a wolf last winter.' That was all that there was for them to say, and it was useless. If old Ffion had not gone beyond the sunset there would have been one more voice raised for him, but it would still have been useless.

Again the murmur was running through the crowd, soft, but fierce, and rising fiercer moment by moment. 'Drive him out!'

Rhiada flung up his head. 'Though he is not of the Tribe by his first birth that brought him into the world, is he not of the Tribe and the Clan and the Men's Side of the Clan by the second birth of his initiation, that brought him into the Spear Brotherhood? We call ourselves a free people; shall he not at least have freedom to speak for himself in this matter?'

'Be it as you say, then; let him speak,' said the Chieftain after a moment.

Six harvests ago Beric had spoken for himself in this circle; he had fought for his place in the Clan, and won. But he knew that the time for fighting had gone by. He made a tiny, hopeless gesture. 'Oh, Elders of my Clan, and you, my Spear Brothers whom I have fought and hunted with from the day that I could crawl, what is there for me to say, save that which my father—my foster father—has said already? I have not broken the laws of the Tribe, for I thought that it was my Tribe also. I have the marks of a wolf's teeth here on my

33

shoulder that I got three moons ago defending your lambing pens. I have been one with you in all things, without thought of another people; and if the Red Crests had come against us I would have stood with you to fling them back. I would have died with you, without question, because you were my own. Bad times have come upon the Clan, as doubtless they have come before and will come again, and you say that it is my doing, because I am a stranger, and you cast me out.' A great choking sob rose in his chest, and he fought it down. ' So be it, then; cast me out. I go to my own people.'

Heedless of the harsh splurge of voices that broke in over the end of his words, he strode forward to the hot verge of the Council Fire, and cast down the bronze and bull's-hide shield clanging into the white ash. Setting his teeth, he took his heron-tufted war-spear and broke it across his knee, and laid the pieces beside it.

Then he turned for the last time to the Chieftain, holding himself erect and braced as though he were another spear in the firelight. ' May I go back to the house-place, to take my leave of Guinear my mother, before I go? '

The Chieftain was still caressing the head of his favourite hound. ' You have until the moon rises,' he said.

Beric turned, and went back up the path that opened for him.

A few moments later he was standing once again in the doorway of the familiar house-place that had been home, and was home no longer. ' I have until moonrise to be away, my mother.' He was not conscious of speaking the words, but he heard them hanging in the smoky air; and Guinear must have heard them also, for she cried out sharply, and hurried to him in the doorway, and put her arms round him as though to hold him back.

' No! Oh no, no! '

He let her draw him to the fire, but stood there, rigid and unresponding, as though he had been a pillar of grey granite, so that after a moment she released him with a little sob, and let her hands drop to her side.

34

'They say it is through me that evil times have come upon the Clan,' he said dully. He was vaguely aware that Cunori had entered behind him and was standing by the doorway, and that Arthmail and Arthgal had appeared from somewhere, frightened and subdued.

His mother put out her hands to him again, her eyes straining in her head. 'What will you do? Where will you go?'

'I will go to my own people,' Beric said.

There was a long silence, and then his mother said in a dry, harsh voice: 'You will need food—food and money; wait, and I will get them.'

While he stood beside the fire, staring blindly down into the flames, she began to move about, gathering dried meat and barley cake and stowing them in a leather bag. She fetched a slender hunting-spear that had been his companion on many game trails; she brought out a new cloak, warm and thick, of her own weaving; and going to the kist in the inner chamber, took from it some money. 'It is Roman money,' she said, as she tied it in a scrap of cloth and added it to the food in the leather bag. 'You will need money in the place that you go to.'

And still Beric stood rigidly beside the fire, watched by the scared boys and uneasy hounds; and Cunori stood in the entrance, peering out. 'The sky grows light to moonrise,' he said, without looking round. 'Are you nearly done?'

'I have done now,' Guinear said, in the same dry, harsh voice. She returned to Beric by the fire. 'Here is food for your journey, and money, and a spear, and a new cloak to keep you warm.'

He took them from her, and flung the cloak round him, and was just stabbing home the pin of the bronze shoulder-brooch when someone else thrust past Cunori in the doorway, and he swung round to see that it was Cathlan, carrying a light hunting-spear.

'I was afraid you would be already gone,' Cathlan said breathlessly. 'It is my best throw-spear, and you will be needing a spear. Take it, Beric.'

35

'I have spears of my own,' Beric said, 'but I take it for the good hunting that we have had together. Do you take this one of mine, for the same reason.'

As the weapons changed hands, Cathlan asked: 'What will you do, among your own people?'

Beric glanced a little uncertainly at the spear in his hand, then up again at the friend who had given it to him. 'Maybe I will join the Eagles.'

For a moment he knew that it was on Cathlan's tongue to say, 'I will go with you.' But the moment passed, and Cathlan said: 'Good hunting to you, my brother.'

'And to you,' Beric said, turning with him to the doorway. For an instant he felt Cathlan's arm hard and heavy across his shoulders; and then his friend was gone, as quickly as he had come.

'The first rim of the moon is above the hills,' said Cunori.

'Bid the moon tarry but for a single heart-beat,' Beric said, and turned again to his mother. 'Guinear, my mother, you do not believe that I have brought trouble upon the Clan?'

'I do not know. I do not care.' Guinear held him close, and his head was down on her shoulder. 'I know only that you have always been my son, my little first-born son, and that I love you. . . .'

'Oh, Mother! Mother!'

'Send me word,' she begged. 'Find means to send me word, one day——'

'One day, when I have made a new life among my own people, I will send you word,' Beric promised. 'Once, that you may know that it is well with me, and then never again. Better you forget that there were ever three sons at the hearth fire.'

'I shall not forget, not the son that was my first-born.' His mother strained him close an instant, then thrust him away. 'The Sun and the Moon be with you, little Cub.'

'And with you, my mother.' Beric stooped for his bundle and the spear that lay beside it. He shook off his weeping brothers and the troubled and bewildered hounds that

36

thronged about him, and thrust through them to the doorway.
Cunori's hand came down on his shoulder, halting him an
instant; and he looked round, seeing the lean red head of the
man who had been his father lit on one side by the friendly
firelight, on the other by the remote silver of the rising moon.
'Already the fever is growing less; there will be good times
again for the Clan,' said Cunori. 'And when the good times
come, they will forget. It may be that in a few years——'
Beric shook his head. 'The Clan has cast me out. If,
when the good times come again, they forget, it would be but
till the next bad harvest. Even you, my father, though you
fought for me down yonder by the Council Fire, are you sure
in your heart that it is not through me that the bad harvest
and the fever came?'

He waited an instant with a faint hope of denial; but Cunori
was a very truthful soul.

'The Gods be good to you, my father,' Beric said, and felt
Cunori's hand slacken and slip from his shoulder as he plunged
out into the young night.

The Council Fire was dying down, but the whole village
was still gathered in the open space and around the gateway
in the stockade. They drew back from him, silent, hostile,
leaving him a wide road; and he strode down it, looking
neither to the right nor left. Here and there they cried out
after him, words for the averting of evil. They crowded in
behind him, and he felt the pressure of their hate thrusting
him out; felt it far more clearly than he heard the rattling of
spear-butts on shields to drive away evil spirits. He refused
to be hurried; he strode steadily on, his shoulders braced and
his head up. He reached the gateway, and passed out
between the turf banks and the thorn hedge where the blossom
showed through the shadows, like foam-curds in a dark wave.
A knot of young warriors thrust into the gateway behind him,
jostling out on his track, giving tongue like a wolf-pack in full
cry; and a flight of stones came whizzing viciously after him.
The light of the rising moon made for uncertain aim, but
even so one caught him in the shoulder and another grazed

37

his cheek. He knew that it was not Beric they were stoning, but the bad harvest and the fever. ' Still,' he thought, ' they need not have thrown stones ! They need not have thrown stones ! ' Another caught him full behind the ear and made him stagger in his tracks. He broke into a stumbling run. The shouting and the shield-drumming were growing fainter behind him; and a last stone, flung at extreme range, thudded into the grass beside him.

' They need not have thrown stones,' he thought dully, over and over again. ' They need not have thrown stones.'

How quiet the field-strips were in the first glimmering of moonlight. Kind, the earth was, kinder than men; the familiar field-strips did not throw stones.

He came to the edge of the oak-woods and, slackening his pace, struck into the game-track that led eastward into the moonrise; eastward toward his own people. Presently he might look for a place to sleep, but hunter that he was, he could travel as well by night as by day, and his one thought was to push on, to get away from the village, as far as ever he could, before he stopped to rest.

There was a sound of flying paws behind him, and the rustle of something slipping low through the undergrowth, and even as he turned to face it, with his hand tightening on his spear-shaft, Gelert brushed by against his leg, circled round, and stood looking up at him, his tail lashing, and the star-shaped blaze on his forehead silver in the moonlight.

Out of his old life, one living thing—Gelert his dog—had kept unswerving faith with him; had come to be with him. The consciousness that he was a warrior with more than half a year of grown manhood behind him, which had stiffened Beric until now, suddenly deserted him. He squatted down, and with his arms round the great dog's neck and his face buried in the thick, harsh hair, he cried as Arthmail, or even Arthgal might have done, while Gelert licked and licked at his bare arm.

But he could not take Gelert with him, not into the Legions; for the Red Crests did not use dogs in war, as the Tribesmen did. After a little while he scrambled to his feet and pointed back the way he had come. 'Home. Go home. We are not hunting to-night, brother,' he said huskily.

The dog stood still. He looked uncertainly in the direction of Beric's pointing finger, and then up into his face, whimpering.

'Home,' Beric said again, and walked on. Gelert padded after him.

Beric halted again, and stooping, turned the dog round to face homeward. 'Home,' he ordered. 'Off! Home, brother!' and pointed his meaning with an open-palmed slap on the brindled rump.

Still Gelert hesitated an instant, then he slunk off a little way, and checked, one paw raised, looking back. But Beric still pointed 'Home! Go Home!' and with drooping tail, Gelert went.

Beric stood in the middle of the track, and watched until the last flicker of the brindled hide was lost in the criss-cross black-and-silver shadow-pattern of the moonlit forest. Then he turned his face once more towards his own people.

IV

THE MEN FROM THE SEA

THREE days later, in the first fading of the spring twilight, Beric stood before the north gateway of Isca Dumnoniorum, watching the few people who still came and went through the archway, wanting to go in himself, but hesitating, wary as a wild animal that scents a trap. The battlemented walls of the frontier town looked unpleasantly strong, as though once inside there might be no getting out again. . . . But that was stupid, of course, and he could not stand here all night. A man went past him leading a string of three ponies with bales of merchandise on their backs, and Beric straightened his shoulders and, joining the tail of the string, followed it in under the massive arch, past the men in leather tunics and steel caps, with long spears in their hands, who stood on guard there.

Just within the gates he came to another halt. So this was a town! A town such as his own people built! His first impression was of straight lines everywhere, straight walls and roof-edges, a long street running away from him straight as a spear-shaft until it lost itself in a confusion of deepening shadows. And the people! The shifting, busy, many-coloured crowd! Beric stood there in bewilderment until he found somebody shouting curses at him, and he had to leap aside to save himself from being run down by a fast mule-carriage sweeping out of a side street.

'Are you deaf?' someone was demanding. 'Or just tired of life?'

The mule-carriage rattled on, the little bells on the harness jingling, and Beric, gathering himself together, decided that the middle of a Roman street was no place in which to stand

and stare. Without more ado, he set off towards the fort, which was his reason for coming to Isca Dumnoniorum, and which he could see rising unmistakably above the end of a short side street.

He turned in towards it, but where the few houses ended under the shoulder of the little hill, halted again, looking up the steep flinted road that lifted between vegetable plots to the gate of the fort. He had seen the fort from a long way outside the town, but somehow it had not looked so large and formidable as it did now: a lean, red, frowning fort, its gate-towers sharp edged against a watered sky. He had meant to go up there to-night, and tell whoever it was that one told these things to that he had come to join the Eagles; but it was growing late, and the light was going fast, and perhaps they would not let him in when once the light was gone. In the gathering shadows the fort seemed to crouch, watchful and faintly menacing, on its hill-top. Perhaps in the morning it would look less dangerous. If he went up there in the morning, it would be just as good as going up now. He had money for a night's lodging—the money that Guinear had given him. He would come back in the morning; and meanwhile he would see something of this strange and wonderful thing that was a town.

Yet still he lingered, irresolute, half minded to go up now, after all, but too lost and bewildered from the events of the last few days to hold steadily to any plan. Behind him he could hear the rise and fall of sound from the town, voices and wheels, hooves and feet, passing and re-passing along the streets—a sound that he had never heard before, and found vaguely exciting. This was the place where the Tribe had risen against the Eagles, a few years before he was born. The Eagles had been too strong for them, and they had been beaten back, with the loss of many men, so that even to-day there were thin places in the Men's Side of the frontier Clans. Well, that was one thing that they could not lay at his door, Beric thought bitterly.

Above him in the fort that had stood firm against that

rising, a trumpet sang out, and he wondered what it meant. To-morrow he would find out.

Meanwhile he turned back to the town. Many lights had pricked out there while he was watching the fort, yellow as dandelions in the dusk, shining from open doorways or from lanterns hanging in porches or at street corners. They cast dim showers of gold across the narrow streets and the passing crowds, and deepened the shadows between light and light to a hazy darkness. Beric was beginning to feel hungry, and very tired, but he did not want to eat or sleep yet; he was too restless.

For a long time he wandered about Isca Dumnoniorum. He found parts of the town that were only half built, so that he realized afresh that this was a new town rising from the blackened ruins of the old one that had been burned down after the rising. He looked in at lamplit shops where they sold red pottery, or loaves, or goldsmith's work that seemed to him most beautiful, or leather goods, or meat. How odd to buy meat instead of hunting for it, he thought. He caught glimpses of lantern-lit courtyards where men strolled about or lounged at tables and women were going round with wine-jars. Those must be wine-shops; he had heard of such places. In one he saw a man sitting, with a great crimson-crested helmet on the bench beside him, and stopped to stare his fill. The soldiers at the gate had had only steel caps with a knob on top; this was his first real Red Crest. Once or twice he caught glimpses through the doorways of people's houses, of the small, sheltered world inside; but from these he turned away quickly, because they hurt him, and wandered on again, watching the people in the streets, men and women, British and Roman, slave and free, gathering sounds and sights and smells to lay in a thick layer over the hurt within him.

Presently he found himself again in the centre of the town, standing on the edge of an open square surrounded by colonnades, from the far side of which rose a building that seemed to him huge almost past believing. Surely some very great man must live in such a great hall; yet there was no light in

42

the few high windows, and somehow the place had an air of being empty. Perhaps the great man was away, and his household with him.

Someone stopped beside him to tighten a slipping sandal-strap by the light of a temple lantern under which he was standing, and Beric turned to him on an impulse, and asked, 'What man lives in there?'

The man, a small, merry-looking individual in a filthy tunic, with a scarlet cap stuck rakishly on the back of his head, straightened up and stared at him with round bright eyes. He looked so blank that Beric thought perhaps he did not speak his tongue, and was just going to try again, more loudly, when the man said, 'In *there*?' jerking a thumb in the direction of the huge building. His voice had the slight nasal twang which Beric came to know later as the accent of Greece.

'Yes. Surely it must be a very great chieftain to live in so great a house.'

'Zeus!' said the man, and laughed. 'No one lives there; that is the Basilica, and all this here in front of it is the Forum.'

'Oh,' said Beric, damped, but still curious. 'What is it for if nobody lives in it?'

'For business,' said the man—'business of all sorts, that is what it's for. It's where the merchants meet—and for everything else that happens in the town. When a robber comes to trial, or a boy to manhood, or a soldier to be honoured, or the townsfolk call a meeting to complain about the drains, it all happens somewhere around the Forum or the Basilica. Where are you sprung from, that you don't know that?'

Beric pointed in his turn towards the north-west. 'Over yonder, three days' trail across the frontier.'

'Down on a trading trip, eh? Skins or hunting dogs?'

The man was obviously friendly, and Beric, who had been feeling more and more lost and lonely all evening, was very glad to find someone to talk to. 'No,' he said. 'I came down to join the Eagles.'

The Greek looked at him with a suddenly arrested eye. 'What a young game-cock! Just you by your lone?'

A bleak shadow passed over Beric's face. 'Just me by my lone.'

'So?' The little man nodded, bright-eyed like a bird. 'And not a friend nor kinsman in the town? You'll have spent a lonely evening, I'm thinking,' he grinned. 'I'm a seaman and a trader myself, and I know those evenings spent kicking your heels round a strange town where you know not a soul and not a soul knows you.'

Beric returned the grin, grateful for the warmth of a human contact as a lost dog for a friendly pat. 'I had meant to go straight up to the fort, but it was dusk when I arrived, and I thought I had maybe better leave it until the morning. Besides, I was minded to look round the town; but it is lonely work on my own, even as you say.'

The little seaman looked at him for a silent and considering moment. 'Have you found yourself a sleeping place for to-night, youngster? No, I'll be bound you haven't.'

'No, I haven't,' Beric admitted. 'Could you tell me of a good place where I could get something to eat, and sleep afterwards? Somewhere that would not cost too much?'

The other shook his head dubiously. 'I'm not so sure that I can. Oh, there are inns and to spare in Isca Dumnoniorum, but they are not over-eager to take in travellers that arrive out of nowhere after dark.' Then his eye brightened as with an idea. 'I'll tell you what, though; the best thing you can do is to come along with me, back to the *Clio*! We are all sleeping on board to-night because we sail with the morning tide, but I daresay you'll not mind being turned out early, and you'll have pleasant quarters and cheerful company for the night. What do you say to that, now?'

'I say that I will come,' Beric said. 'I will come very gladly.' He pushed himself off from the column against which he had been leaning, suddenly aware of his leaden weight of weariness.

'Well said! I like a lad who can make up his mind without

44

arguing. Down this way; we will go to the Golden Tree first
—the rest of us will be there, and whatever the state of your
belly, mine is as empty as a wine-skin after Saturnalia.'

Beric went with him thankfully down the sloping street to
the West Gate, the River Gate, which was still open, though the
other gates of the town had been shut since dark. 'The
River Gate stays open most of the night; that's because half
the town is outside it,' his companion told him. And after a
cheerful exchange of insults with the guard, in the unknown
tongue which most of Isca Dumnoniorum seemed to speak—
but that would be Latin, of course, the tongue of his own
people—they passed out through the narrow, lantern-lit
archway.

The half of the town outside the River Gate was not the
respectable half; that was clear even to Beric; but as they
plunged into the maze of narrow ways, instantly he was more
at home than he had been in the respectable half within the
walls. It was a mere huddle of turf-and-timber bothies
between the town walls and the river, dark save for the occasional gleam of a fire-lit doorway. Poor quarter; seamen's
quarter, but also native quarter; and mingled with the other
smells, the familiar smell of wood-smoke and horse-droppings
about it, that was the smell of home.

Only a few steps from the gate, his new friend, whose name
he had by that time discovered was Aristobulo, dived like a
rabbit into a dark gash between the crowding hovels, at the
end of which Beric caught the silver glint of the river; and
half-way down, turned again, into a dimly lighted doorway.
Beric followed him across what appeared to be a stable, and
out through another doorway into a courtyard lit by several
hanging lanterns, and stood blinking in the flood of thick
yellow radiance. There were a dozen or more men in the
courtyard, lounging at their ease on the benches and round the
walls, who greeted Aristobulo noisily, and looked with quick
curiosity at Beric. One of them asked a question half under
his breath in the Latin tongue.

Aristobulo, shouldering into their midst, answered in the

same tongue, and then changed quickly to the Celtic, for Beric's benefit. 'Look now, lads. I've brought back a friend—Beric, his name is—and he's minded to join the Eagles to-morrow, and maybe rise to Emperor, like many a one before him; but he's got nothing to do and nowhere to go for the night, so he might as well spend it with us.'

Several of the men laughed, as though something in this struck them as funny; and Beric wondered what it was. He thought perhaps it was the reference to the Emperor. But whatever it was, they nodded to him in friendly fashion, and one of them, who seemed to be their chief, said: 'Any friend of yours, Aristobulo,' while another made room for them on a bench in the corner; and in a very short time, not quite sure how it all happened, Beric found himself sitting on the bench, helping himself out of a bowl of stewed goat's-flesh which a stout woman in a pink tunic and a great deal of glass jewellery had brought out and set between him and his new friend Aristobulo. The fat woman poured wine for him into an earthen cup, and he drank it because he was thirsty; but he did not like it very much, not as much as heather beer, not even as much as milk.

Now that his eyes were used to the light, and he had leisure to look about him, he saw that the building that enclosed the courtyard was reed-thatched like a British house-place; but right across one plastered wall there was daubed in yellow paint a sprawling tree—that was why the place was called the Golden Tree, he supposed—with many birds in its branches, oddly shaped birds, but jewel-coloured. He was free to look at the men around him, too, for they were talking together in their own tongue while they ate and drank, leaving him for the moment to himself.

They were lean men, with a ranging, winter-wolf air about them, and eyes that looked used to long distance. They wore short tunics and loose short cloaks, much stained and faded, and several of them had close-fitting caps such as the one Aristobulo wore. The chief among them, who seemed to be called Phanes, was a very tall man, powerfully and beautifully

46

built, who fascinated Beric because his close, curled beard was dyed vermilion and he wore gold drops in his ears like a woman. He was so unlike anything that Beric had seen before that he sat staring at him with the wheat-cake and strong cheese that had followed the stew untouched in his hand, until the tall man, looking round for the woman of the house to refill his cup, caught the stare. Beric flushed up to the roots of his hair, but Phanes only laughed, with a fierce, merry flash of white teeth in his vermilion beard, and lifted his empty cup to him. Beric lifted his own in reply, but something in the other's snapping laughter made him faintly uneasy; all at once, so deep down in his mind that he was scarcely aware of it, a little warning hammer began to beat. 'Danger! danger!' He was not quite sure that he trusted these men.

He thrust the doubt away as base ingratitude to Aristobulo, who had been friendly to him in this town of strangers. And then Aristobulo himself, who had been deep in argument with a barrel-chested man beside him, turned to draw Beric into the talk. Wonderful talk it was, too, when they changed their tongue for his benefit and he could understand it— shining talk that they tossed from one to another like a bright ball: of sea-monsters and sea-fights and voyages whole moons out of sight of land. One man, it seemed, had sailed half the world over in search of a magical golden fleece, and had the most incredible adventures on the way; while Aristobulo himself told of birds with heads like beautiful women, whose sweet singing lured seamen to their deaths.

'I suppose,' said Aristobulo, looking round at his comrades and from them to Beric—'I do suppose as I am the only man save one that has heard that song and lived. It was this way. Ye see, the Captain I was serving with—not Phanes—was a very wily man, and when he knew that we were drawing near to the island where these Syrens sing, he gave orders that all of us were to stop our ears with beeswax, that we might not hear, while he was bound to the mast and his ears left free, so that he might hear the song but not go to it. So it was done, and we held to our course, and by and by we sees the island in the distance, and then we sees by the Captain's face that he's begun to hear the song. Lit up, it did, like as if he saw his heart's desire before him. And then he began to struggle to get free of his bonds, but they was too surely tied; pull and strain at them he did, and we could see him crying out to us to untie him, but a' course we couldn't hear nothing. Presently we come close alongside the island: little and low it was, and flowery, and there on it stood the three Syrens, like great birds and their heads as the heads of women with long golden hair. And all among the little bright flowers there was bones a-lying—the bleached white bones of sailor men! Now the beeswax in my left ear weren't stuffed home as surely as it should a' been, and suddenly a trickle of the song that the Syrens were singing got through—faint like the sea in a shell, it was, but 'twas enough! I pulls out the bit of wax, and the song comes flooding in, so sweet as never mortal song in this world, and up I jumps to fling myself overboard and go to it, for I hadn't got no choice. But my mate sees what's in the wind, and he ups with his fist and catches me such a blow under the ear that I goes out like a candle. And the next thing I know, the island is only a shadow in our wake, and the Captain sitting on the deck and sobbing like a babe.' Aristobulo wagged his head sadly. 'But there's times when I wish I'd never heard that song: comes between me and my vittles, now and again, it do.'

'But not to-night, eh lad?' said the barrel-chested man, with an eye on the cheese, and there was a general laugh; and another man put in: 'Talking of cheese—that minds me of the time . . .'

So it went on. And as Beric listened, gradually the little warning hammer beat softer and softer yet; and ceased to beat at all.

Presently Phanes lounged to his feet, stretching until the little muscles cracked behind his shoulders. 'Time we got back to the ship, lads,' he said. 'Herope and Castor will be growing tired of being left in sole charge of the live-stock.'

48

'What live-stock is that?' Beric asked his new friend curiously, as they all struggled to their feet.

'Only a few leash of hunting dogs being shipped to Rome, and some poultry for the voyage. The hounds fight if they get a chance,' said Aristobulo.

The men who were nearest to them, and caught his words, glanced at each other with a glint of laughter. And again Beric wondered why; and again the little warning woke and beat in his brain. 'Danger! danger!' But it was gone again almost before it came.

The men were settling their scores with the fat woman in pink, but when Beric brought out his few coins she patted his arm with a podgy brown hand, looking at him out of eyes rimmed with black stibium, that must once have been beautiful and said: 'Nay now, Honey. *They* have seen to all that.'

For an instant her hand tightened on his arm, as though she was half minded to hold him back to say something to him, but Aristobulo was calling to him to come on, and with a quick word of thanks, he hurried to join his new friend at the courtyard entrance. 'Aristobulo, she says you paid for me— I did not mean——'

'Why, lad, I don't ask a friend to supper and expect him to pay!' Aristobulo grinned companionably, and flung an arm round Beric's shoulder and swept him off after the rest.

They strolled in a bunch down the twisting alleyway, exchanging a passing word here and there with others of their kind, and came out on the river bank, where a rough jetty thrust out into the water. And, lying alongside, was the first ship that Beric had ever seen at close quarters. The *Clio* was a battered little tub, a fine sea vessel, but not beautiful, save with that beauty which comes with absolute fitness for the use for which a thing was created. But to Beric, seeing her in the moonlight, dark against the fish-scale silver of the river save for the tawny glow of a brazier at her stern, the furled sail on her yard like a folded wing against the sky, she seemed unbelievably strange and mysterious, a creature of the sea, part

49

gull, part dolphin, lying asleep on the bright surface of the water.

A plank ran from the jetty, over the ship's side, and the men were crowding up it. Beric followed, sniffing for the first time the mingled smell of rope and pitch and salt-soaked timber which was the smell of ships; and Aristobulo brought up the rear. Two men who had been sitting by the brazier uncoiled themselves and got up, and there was a rapid exchange of question and answer between them and Phanes, as they glanced at Beric. Some of the crew gathered round the brazier, others remained leaning over the side to talk to a couple of tribesmen on the bank; and Beric, with the living sensation of the deck beneath his feet, stood looking round him wide-eyed at the moon-washed curve of the high stern, at the stout mast rising up and the dark wing-curve of the furled sail against the glimmering sky.

Then Aristobulo touched him on the arm. ' If you've stared your fill, 'tis time we were turning in, for the morning tide turns seaward early. Down the hatch, here.'

And Beric noticed for the first time a square patch of blackness in the moon-whitened deck, just before the mast; a square hole, and a ladder leading down into the dark belly of the sea monster. It reminded him uncomfortably of the mouth of a trap, but of course that was simply foolishness, and Aristobulo, whose salt he had eaten, was already disappearing down it. ' Come down backwards,' Aristobulo called. ' You are the less likely to break your neck. It is as black as Erebus down here, but we'll get a light before you can sneeze.'

Beric hesitated an instant longer, then slipped over the edge of the hole, found the rungs, and dropped downward. The seamen by the bulwarks were still talking and laughing with the tribesmen on the bank. Below him, out of the darkness, rose a faint sense of life, a breathy, formless rustling, something that might have been a groan, and the thick smell of too many people packed in too small a space, not hounds or poultry; a human smell. It was very odd.

50

Suddenly the little warning hammer began to beat again, sharp and urgent this time. 'Danger! danger!' His feet had just found the lower deck, and the moonlit sky was a glimmering square level with the top of his head, as he sprang for it again—too late. There was a swift movement behind him, and in that same instant something seemed to burst in the back of his head, and he stumbled forward into a spinning blackness shot with coloured lights.

V

THE ARM-RING

Hᴵɢн overhead the white, high-piled clouds drifted
slowly before the early autumn wind across a sky of
speedwell blue, but down below in the principal slave-
market of Rome there seemed no air at all. It was still
early in the day, but already the market was crowded, as
always. Here a master builder moved purposefully between
the pens, looking for a good strong human animal to carry
stones and mix concrete; there a stout matron looking for a
girl to spin and carry cushions, and getting very hot and
flustered about it; a senator in search of a secretary; a young
Tribune wanting a body-slave; a grey-haired steward of a
great household—himself a slave—making careful choice of a
new under-cook to replace one that had just died. A many-
coloured, many-voiced, shifting throng that came and went
and came again, up and down the lanes between the pens and
pitches where the slaves that they were seeking waited to be
bought.

In the corner of one such pen, Beric sat on the hard, hot
pavement with his arms across his knees, staring straight before him. Some of his companions spoke to each other from
time to time, but mostly they sat silent, as listless and hopeless
as himself. Aaron Ben Malachi, whose property they were,
leaned against a temple column that formed the corner of his
pitch, discussing prices with his neighbour. Prices were bad,
it seemed. 'A big fine Athenian, gently born and played
upon the lyre like an angel, and I had to let him go for three
thousand sesterces! Only last week that was. Ai, ai, ai, I
shall be ruined if the market does not improve!' Beric heard
the long complaint going on and on; he saw the feet of the
passers-by moving in front of him: dusty sandals, military

53

boots, the pretty scarlet slippers of a lady of rank, the bare
blistered feet of a beggar; but he was not thinking of what he
heard or saw. He was wondering—how long was it since that
night at Isca Dumnoniorum? Five moons? Six? Seven?
He did not know, he had lost count long ago. He knew only
that they had been the moons of a nightmare, such a nightmare as one wakes from with the taste of evil in one's mouth.
Sometimes he thought that that was what it really was, an ill
dream from which he might awake at any moment; but the
waking never came.

After that night in Isca Dumnoniorum he had woken to
find himself in the belly of the strange sea-beast that was a
ship, lying with several others of his kind, in what space remained between the piled bales of the cargo. The *Clio* was
at sea, and they had all been very sick. Most of the others had
been bought perfectly legally from Roman landowners along
the south coast, but two beside himself had been carried off,
and one of these, who had been captured while out fishing,
seemed to find a certain comfort for himself in explaining the
whole hideous situation to Beric and inquiring whether he had
never heard of Greek slavers and their ways. The slavers
themselves had met his furious protests and rebellion with a
few floggings and a certain amount of knocking about; not
too much, for it was in their interest to get the cargo in
reasonably good condition to its destination, but sufficient to
school him. And Beric's hands became quivering fists as he
remembered their schooling. He was living again the
misery of those past moons. Sold and resold from one trader
to another, like a dressed skin or a cooking-pot; the filthy
Tiber-side sheds where he had been herded with slaves of every
colour and smell, all his brothers and sisters in misery; the
scanty food, the kicks and blows of the slave-drivers; above
all, the sense of utter helplessness, of being caught and caged
and lost to all eternity.

A little cur dog, scavenging among the feet of the crowd,
slunk past him, and he stretched out a hand to it. It sniffed
his fingers, fawned for an instant with flattened ears under his

touch, and then slunk away. There was one thing he had to be thankful for, anyway, he thought, watching it out of sight: that he had not had Gelert with him that night. What would have become of Gelert, left alone in a strange town—always supposing that he had not been knifed by the slavers? At the thought of Gelert a wave of blinding misery swept over Beric. His Tribe, his father and mother, even Cathlan, he had shut away from him; but his dog, that was another matter.

There was a sudden stir around him. A pretty, bold-looking girl, with a crimson edge to her tunic and a gold chain round her neck, had come up and was speaking to Ben Malachi, who had abandoned his column and come forward, smiling hopefully and rubbing his hands together, to receive her orders.

'My mistress, the Lady Julia,' said the girl, with a gesture of her head towards a richly curtained litter carried on the shoulders of six men, which had halted a few paces off, 'needs a replacement for one of her Gaulish litter-bearers. Have you anything that might do? It must be something good; only the best will serve for my Lady.'

Beric, who had picked up a good many words of Latin by now (though he no longer thought of it as the tongue of his own people), understood what she said well enough, but paid no heed, since he was not Gaulish, and therefore it could have nothing to do with him.

But Ben Malachi was not one to let slip the chance of a sale for so small a matter as that. 'I have the very slave to suit the Lady Julia, the best—oh, yes, indeed; would I think for one moment, my dear, of trying to sell anything but the best to so great a lady?' He made a quick gesture to his slave-driver, a slant-eyed Syrian, who promptly kicked Beric with a nailed sandal.

'Up, you.'

Beric stumbled to his feet without protest; he was well used to kicks by now, and followed Ben Malachi and the girl towards the curtained litter.

The curtain was drawn back a little now, and the lady

inside was talking to a tall man with the purple stripe of a senator down his tunic, who had just paused to greet her. ' He took to brawling, so of course I had to sell him, and put Philo in his place for the present,' Beric heard a clear, musical voice saying. ' But you may see for yourself that it completely *ruins* my matched team.' Then as the little group came up: ' Ah, Ben Malachi, have you brought me something? '

The curtain was drawn back farther, and Beric found himself looking at the woman within. A beautiful woman, but cold, so cold. She looked him over with careless eyes that never noticed that he was human, and scarcely seemed to listen to Ben Malachi's list of his good points. Then she shook her head. ' No, no, he will not do. I must have a Gaul.'

' This one is British, my Lady; the same stock——' the slave merchant began, bowing; but she cut him short.

' He is too dark and too red. I must have a golden Gaul, or spoil my team.'

' As to the colour of his hair, noble lady '—Ben Malachi was bending almost double—' might I suggest a few lime-washes, a very few——'

This time it was the man with the Senator's stripe on his tunic who cut in, saying lazily: ' Julia, you cannot do that! Percol! It would be like faking a chestnut to make a matched chariot team with bays.'

' My dear Hirpinius, you may make your mind easy: I have no intention of doing it,' said the Lady Julia with bored amusement, then to Ben Malachi, ' unless you can show me something else, I must leave the matter for now, or try elsewhere.'

' In a few days, but three at the most, I shall have some fresh stock.' Ben Malachi bowed again, his thin grey beard flapping up and down on the breast of his black robe. ' Very fine stock! If the most gracious lady permits, I will send along any that seem suitable for her inspection before anyone else sees them. I am a poor man and——'

' As you will. I may look at them if I have found nothing

to suit me in the meantime,' said the most gracious lady.
'Hirpinius, do you walk my way? No? Until our next
meeting, then.' She made a gesture to her golden Gauls:
the embroidered curtain fell back into place, and the litter-
bearers moved off, carrying their burden, with the maid
walking beside it.

Beric was herded back into the pen, and squatted hopelessly down again in his corner.

The hours dragged by, and in the crowded slave-market
there seemed less and less air to breathe. Three of his fellow-
slaves were sold. One of them, a big negro, had been friendly,
and if it were possible for Beric to feel more desolate than he
did already, he would have done so as he watched the broad
black figure follow his new master away. Long past noon,
when the slave-market was almost deserted and the pave-
ments threw back the heat like the blast from an oven, a man
came by, glanced at Beric, hesitated, and came back. He was
a young man with a broad, pleasant face, and carried himself
as though used to the weight of a soldier's harness. He spoke
to Ben Malachi, but his gaze remained on Beric, and meeting
it, Beric was filled with a sudden desperate hope, and got up
without waiting to be kicked to his feet by the slave-driver.

'How much do you want for him?' the young man was
asking, cutting short Ben Malachi's usual flow of praise for his
wares.

'Only two thousand sesterces, Centurion.'

'One thousand,' said the young man.

'The centurion makes a jest.' Ben Malachi spread his
hands and smiled. 'Nineteen hundred, my dear.'

'Eleven hundred.'

The bargaining was so quick and quiet that Beric could
scarcely follow it, but he understood all too clearly when at
last the young man said with a little gesture of finish:

'Thirteen hundred and fifty. I can go no higher.'

'Seventeen hundred,' said the Jew. 'You will not get a
good strong slave to take with you into Dacia for less than that
anywhere, my dear.'

57

'Then I must needs go without one.'

'Sixteen hundred and fifty—take him for sixteen hundred and fifty!' wailed Ben Malachi. 'And may it never come between you and sleep that you have ruined an old man!'

'I cannot go beyond thirteen fifty; I have not got it,' said the young man, already turning away. Over his shoulder he looked back. 'I am sorry,' he said, not to Ben Malachi, but to Beric himself. Then he was gone: and Beric, feeling suddenly sick, sat down again.

More time crawled by. Two more of Ben Malachi's slaves found purchasers. The westering sun slanted across the slave-market, which had become crowded again; and still Beric sat in his corner, where the stones were beginning to cool in the widening shade. He was no longer thinking, just sitting, with his elbows on his knees and his aching head in his hands, while still the feet of the throng moved by: saffron shoes of a priest, nailed sandals of a gladiator. . . . He was roughly jerked out of the half stupor into which he had sunk, to find that another purchaser had appeared. Thrust forward by the heavy hand of the slave-driver, he found himself standing before a small stout man with a puckered pink face, and hot-tempered eyes of very faded blue which were looking him up and down exactly as they might have studied the points of a pony—save that probably they would have had more of kindness in them for a pony.

After the first glance, his head went down, and he stood with stubborn, hunched shoulders, and wide-planted feet, staring at the small man's stomach, which was round and pompous.

'Is this the best you have?' the small man was demanding.

'I have a very pretty Syrian boy, Excellency——'

'The whole market is full of pretty Syrian boys. I have had them before, and they thieve like monkeys.' Excellency sounded both tired and exasperated.

A depressed-looking man hovering just behind him said anxiously, 'If you would allow me to attend to the matter to-morrow, sir.'

'If I required anyone to choose the household slaves for me, it would be my steward's job, not my secretary's,' said his master waspishly. 'I *always* choose my own slaves: you should know that by now. No, I said I would replace Damon to-day, and I am a man of my word.' Then to Ben Malachi: 'Apart from the Syrian, *is* that the best you have?'

The Jew bowed again. 'He is a very fine boy, Excellency, worthy even of the household of Publius Lucianus Piso the Magistrate. Unbroken, yes, but intelligent; ai, ai, ai, your steward could train him to anything in half a month.'

'He is sullen,' said Publius Piso.

'He is new to slavery. The British do not take easily to the arm-ring; but a few whippings will soon remedy that.' Ben Malachi made a sign to his slave-driver, who promptly thrust a hand under Beric's chin to force it up. The boy flung his head back from the man's touch, and stood staring, straight enough now, into the round pink face before him.

'British, is he?' said the Magistrate.

'British indeed, Excellency, and a chieftain's son, as like as not, in his own country.'

The Magistrate grunted. 'Every barbarian slave is a chieftain's son in his own country if you and your kind are to be believed. More likely he's the son of a renegade legionary, by his build.' He hesitated. 'Still, I like the look of him. He is healthy?'

'Oh, he is indeed, Excellency; you would not find a healthier boy.'

'Hmm,' said Publius Piso, and reached out to feel the boy's arm. Beric started as though he had been stung, then stood rigid, frowning from the plump pink hand on his arm to the plump pink face of its owner, and back again. 'Good muscle,' said the Magistrate approvingly. 'Breathe in.'

Beric stared at him between bewilderment and outrage, but a cuff from the slave-driver pointed the demand, and he breathed in; breathed in until he felt his chest must burst. His hands had become quivering fists, but no one seemed aware of that. 'Hmm,' said the Magistrate again. 'Open your mouth.'

And so it went on.

'He seems sound enough,' the round pink man admitted at last. 'I still say he is sullen, though. He didn't like it when I looked him over. You will have to take something off the price for that.'

The Jew spread his hands. 'Does one lower the price of a colt for the fire there is in him?'

'I want a slave, not a colt,' Publius Piso said shortly. 'How much do you want for him?'

'Two thousand six hundred sesterces, Excellency.'

'Fifteen hundred.'

The bargaining began again. But this time it ended with agreement reached. Beric's papers changed hands, and at a word from his master the secretary paid over the purchase money into the eager palms of Aaron Ben Malachi, who received it bowing again and again. 'The noble Publius Piso will never regret his bargain, and when next he has need to buy a slave, it may be that he will remember——'

'Yes, yes, I daresay.' The Magistrate was already turning away. 'Send him up some time this evening. You know the house.'

'Who does not know the house of Publius Lucianus Piso the Magistrate?'

. . . . .

So a little later, having been given a large bowl of lentil porridge, lest he should seem unduly hungry when he arrived, Beric was following one of Ben Malachi's own slaves through the streets of Rome on the way to the home of his new owner. Lest he should try to break away, there was a running noose round his neck, and the slave in charge of him held the other end of it. 'You don't turn difficult, and I don't jerk this rope, see?' said the man.

But Beric was beyond turning difficult, anyway.

They climbed steadily out of the lower city, with its ceaseless, shifting crowds and the faint, sickly smell that Beric knew by now for the smell of the summer plague, into quieter streets and fresher air. They came at last to a gateway in a high wall, and passed through, with the exchange of a few words between the porter and Ben Malachi's slave. Beric was standing in a wide courtyard already growing shadowy in the fading light, and people were swarming in as it seemed from every side, to gather round him, pointing and staring and asking questions that he could not find enough Latin to answer. Then someone who seemed to be in authority joined the group and spoke to Ben Malachi's man, and quite suddenly Ben Malachi's man had slipped off the halter and gone his way.

Left alone in the strange courtyard, Beric had one moment of blind panic. Ben Malachi's man had been a brute, but at least he had been a familiar brute; and now he was gone. Two girls in the group nudged each other, giggling. 'We shan't be keeping this one long,' said one of them. 'He's soft in the head—just look at him.'

'You have no call to laugh at him, even if he is, Tina,' said another, more kindly.

'Best get him cleaned up before Nigellus sees him,' said a third.

And an impatient voice snapped at Beric himself. 'Well, don't stand there all night, looking like a mooncalf.'

He heard them woollenly, through the throbbing in his head. And then he was stumbling across the courtyard and along a passage-way after someone's broad back. The broad back led him to a place where there was a plunge-bath, and he pulled off his filthy rags and got in, slowly and carefully, like an old man. The cold water felt wonderful on his hot, dirt-parched skin, and the chill of it seemed to clear his head; and he scrubbed himself with silver sand, and soaked, and scrubbed again. It was good to feel clean after so many moons.

He stayed in the plunge-bath until the slave who had brought him there came back and demanded to know whether he thought he was a fish; and then he got out and rubbed himself down and pulled on the tunic which the man tossed to him —a tunic of unbleached wool, soft and clean—and followed him out. His own stinking rags they left on the bath-house

62

floor, to be collected and burned by anybody who happened to feel like it, if anyone ever did. That, Beric was to realize later, was typical of the house of Piso.

Without any clear idea of how he got there, he found himself in a small lamp-lit room, standing before a thin grey man, who sat looking at him appraisingly across a table littered with tablets and papyrus rolls. 'Ah yes, the new slave,' said the man in tones of quiet authority. He glanced at a tablet in his hand. 'Your name is Beric?'

'Yes,' said Beric hoarsely.

The grey man wrote it down on a scroll before him. 'So. My name is Nigellus, and I am the steward of this household. You will take most of your orders from me.'

Beric said 'Yes' again.

Nigellus let the scroll fly back on itself abruptly. 'Panteon will find you somewhere to sleep, and the cook will give you a meal if you are hungry. But first——' He took up something from the table before him, and held it out. 'See if this will go over your elbow. If not, I have a larger one.'

Beric took it from him. It was a broad silver arm-ring, stamped with a badge of some sort; and he stared at it stupidly, holding it between his hands as though he did not know what to do with it.

'It is the badge of the house of Piso,' said the steward. 'All Publius Piso's slaves wear such an arm-ring. Put it on, and go.'

Without a word, Beric ran the thing up his left forearm and began to work it over his elbow. It was a tight fit, but he managed it at last, and looked up again, just as the grey man reached out to set aside the scroll in which he had entered the new slave's name: and saw, half revealed by the updrawn sleeve, the rim of just such another arm-ring sparkling in the lamplight.

His gaze jerked up to the steward's face, and encountered a faint flicker in his eyes that might have been amusement or bitterness. 'Oh yes, I also,' said Nigellus.

VI

A FRIEND AND AN ENEMY

FOR the first few days that he wore the Piso arm-ring Beric lived in a state of perpetual bewilderment, so that his head felt hot all the time, and nothing and nobody seemed quite real. And then, very slowly, he began to get his breath back and be able to look about him. His head stopped feeling hot, and he began to learn his way about the courts of the great house on the Viminal Hill, where at first he had got constantly lost, and through the unfamiliar pattern of the days, and even which were which of his fellow slaves.

There were many slaves in the household of Publius Piso, and they all had a tendency to do bits and pieces of each other's work, while somebody else did theirs—or did not, as the case might be. That was not Nigellus's fault; it was partly because the Lady Poppaea was in the habit of calling to any slave she saw and ordering him to drop what he was doing and run instantly and do something else; partly because Publius Piso changed his slaves so often that there were always some in the household who did not know their jobs. Publius Piso was forever buying and selling slaves; Beric soon learned that. The only one who seemed safe from that habit of his was Nigellus. Nigellus had been his body-slave when they were both boys, had gone with him through his Tribune Service with the Legions, and risen slowly to be the steward of his household, and had become so much a part of him that he would as soon have thought of selling his own right arm.

At first Beric wondered why none of the slaves ran away. It would have been quite easy, for they were often sent on errands into the city, and sometimes they had time off, and could go out and spend it as they chose. And then he realized that it was because most of them knew no other life, and for the few like himself who did, there was nowhere to run to. To run away would mean going underground, perhaps joining the robbers, to live at all. There was little future in that.

At least he was no longer hungry, nor beaten without cause.

Officially he was a house slave, but it was not long before he began to find his way into the stables. He liked old Hippias, who had charge there, and who liked him in return; and with the horses—Publius Piso kept fine horses and did not sell them as often as he did his slaves—he was less lonely than with his fellow slaves.

His world was a slave's world, ruled by Nigellus, and the family he served were figures moving in another world, seen at a distance. Publius Piso was a fussy man, but under the fuss and the self-importance a kindly man, who might even have been kind to his slaves if it had occurred to him that they had feelings. His wife, the Lady Poppaea, was a very different matter; fat and white and fretful, and without kindness. The Lady Lucilla was her mother over again, though not fretful. But that, Beric thought, was probably because she was only fifteen. Maybe the Lady Poppaea had not been fretful when she was fifteen. And then there was Glaucus; Glaucus, with his gay good looks and his lazy, laughing manner, standing out from his family like a goldfinch among sparrows.

So Beric saw them, coloured but flat, like figures in a fresco, those first few months that he belonged to them.

The autumn rains had broken soon after he joined the household and the winter came, and there was snow on the Alban Hills, that he could glimpse from an upper window of the slaves' quarters. And then the snow went, and the first faint promise of spring began to stir. And Beric's longing for his own hills and his freedom, that had never left him for a moment, grew quick and urgent within him. 'It must be so that the wild geese feel when they fly north in the spring,' he thought, 'and the swallows when they come from the south to nest under our eaves. But the swallows and the wild geese are free to go when they hear the call.' It was all the worse, in a way, because by that time he was allowed outside the gates, and even, with one or two others, sent out sometimes to exercise the horses; and it would have been so easy to escape, only there was nowhere to escape to.

Then came a morning when the promise of spring was suddenly fulfilled as with a fanfare of trumpets; a morning when the hazels would be flinging their yellow pollen to the wind along the wood-shores of the north, and the curlews would be calling. And something within Beric seemed beating and beating for freedom, until he felt bruised with its beating.

But he was not the only one to feel the spring that morning, for the Lady Lucilla, who always had breakfast in her sleeping-cell in the usual way, suddenly decided to have it in the garden. It so happened that Beric entered the kitchen just as the tray was ready, and the cook thrust it into his hands, saying: ' It is for the young lady. Take it out to her, there's a good lad. She's on the terrace.'

Carefully carrying the tray set with little hot loaves and wild honey, Beric made his way across the inner court with its fountains and its lemon and myrtle trees in slender stone jars, and out into the small garden. The shadow of a flying bird darted before him over the grass, and in the brown shade of the ilex tree beside the terrace steps were a host of tiny pink flowers that looked as though they too were winged and might take flight at any moment.

The Lady Lucilla was sitting on the curved stone bench in a kind of bay of the parapet, with nothing but sky beyond her, for the garden of the Piso house was on the very brow of the Viminal, and beyond the terrace the hill dropped steeply to the heart of Rome. She was playing with a small white kitten with golden eyes, and did not look up at the sound of Beric's sandals on the pavement.

Beric hesitated, wondering suddenly whether he ought to have put the tray down somewhere and brought out a table first; he did not know; it was the first time he had actually

66

waited on any of the family. ' My Lady,' he began at last,
' may I put this on the bench, while I fetch a table? '

She looked up at him. ' Oh, it is you, Beric. Yes, set
the tray here beside me. I shall not want a table.'

Beric bent and set the tray carefully where she bade him,
poured water into the silver cup and shifted the napkin so that
it was towards her hand; and straightened again to find her
still watching him. ' You did that very well,' she said.

' Thank you, my Lady.' Beric stood straight before her,
waiting to be dismissed.

But Lucilla did not dismiss him. Instead she said: ' I saw
you bring back the new Icenian mare from exercise yesterday.'
And then, as he did not answer: ' You are British, too, are
you not? '

' I——' Beric began, and hesitated, gazing at the parapet
behind her. ' I am from Britain.'

Lucilla did not seem to notice the hesitation. After a
moment she said with a small contented sigh, ' Isn't it lovely
that it is spring again? The cyclamen are all coming into
flower under the ilex tree, and soon the swallows will be back
. . . Do you have swallows in Britain, in the spring? '

Beric's gaze slipped away over the parapet into the faint
opal mist of the morning, out of which the hills of Rome rose
into the sunlight. But they were other hills that he was
seeing. ' Yes, we have swallows in Britain, in the spring.'

The Lady Lucilla bent her head quickly over the kitten in
her lap, then looked up again and said with a catch in her
voice: ' That was stupid of me. I am sorry—I did not think.'

Beric stared at her in surprise, at the warmth in her voice
as much as her words. ' My Lady, it—it makes no difference.
I was remembering the swallows already, this morning.'

' Were you? I am so sorry,' said the Lady Lucilla again.

There was an uncertain silence. Beric shifted his weight
from one foot to the other, realizing that she knew no more
than he did what to say next, or how to break off the small,
half-shy exchange that had somehow taken them both unawares.

67

Finally he said: ' My Lady, would you rather have cheese than honey? Shall I bring some? '

She shook her head. ' No, I like honey best. Thank you for bringing me my breakfast, Beric.'

A few moments later, making his way back to the house, with the ache of his misery suddenly a little warmed and comforted, Beric was thinking to himself that the Lady Lucilla was not in the least like her mother, after all. The Lady Poppaea was fat and white and without kindness, but the Lady Lucilla had been kind to a homesick slave, and she no longer looked fat or white to him.

Spring passed by, with its sudden downpours that the sun and the mistral dried almost as they fell, and the lemon-blossom scattered its petals into the cool waters of the fountain, and the long, breathless days of summer came; and it was more than a year since Beric's old life had cast him out. Usually, he found, the household moved out for the hot months to the Piso farm in the Alban hills, but this year they remained in Rome, because the Lady Lucilla was to be married at the summer's end, and there was so much to do, to make ready for the marriage. The Lady Lucilla was marrying a friend and fellow magistrate of her father's, Valarius Longus by name. Beric had seen him sometimes when he came to the house: a lean, dark man, who bore the traces of his early soldiering far more clearly than Publius Piso did. There was a quiet, finely-tempered air about him, and presumably Lucilla liked him, for she seemed well content; but he must be nearly as old as her father, and Beric could not help wondering whether she was as content as she seemed. As the Lady Lucilla had cared whether he was homesick, so he cared whether she was happy.

But Beric had little leisure for wondering, that summer. Only a few days after he first heard about the coming marriage, Bucephalus, the big roan charger, was stung by a gadfly while Hippias was combing his tail, and gave the old man a kick as the result of which he was now laid up with a broken leg, and Beric found himself doing all he could to fill his place for him, so that Publius Piso should not buy another groom. Hippias could not be sold off while he had a broken leg, because naturally no one would buy him; but it was quite possible that Publius Piso might buy another slave now, and if he liked the new one best, sell Hippias the instant he was saleable. Hippias was frightened of that. He was growing old, getting to the stage when a change of masters was almost bound to mean a change for the worse. And squatting beside the pallet bed at the end of the men's dormitory, where the old man lay frightened and in pain, Beric had reassured him as best he could. 'If there is no need for a new groom, it will not come into our master's mind to buy one; not with the Lady Lucilla's marriage to think about. And there *will* be no need for a new groom. I will see to that.' And he had gone to Nigellus and asked to be taken off house duties for the time being. And Nigellus had done his best, so that now nearly all Beric's time was passed in the stables.

He was there one breathless August evening, seeing to Venetia, the Icenian mare, whom the master of the house had just had out. Publius Piso rode for exercise before dinner every other day, unless business prevented him or the weather was too bad. He was not a big man, but he rode heavily and hardly, and to-day Venetia was clearly distressed. Beric did not wonder. There had been a storm brewing all day, brassy clouds banked round the sky-line, and the air heavy and sour with thunder. In the shadowed stable, with every door open, there seemed no air to breathe, and out in the stable yard beyond the door the heat danced above a shimmering mirage that looked like pools of water on the cobbles. The mare hung her head, dribbling and uneasy. The master might have fore-gone his ride to-day, Beric thought. But the master was a man of habit. At least he might have taken Bucephalus, who was better up to his springless thumping. Beric talked to her, softly and consolingly in the Celtic tongue, as he rubbed her down and covered her with the light cloths that would keep her from getting chilled. 'Poor little sister—beautiful sister—it is better now. . . . Yes, I know you are

69

thirsty; you shall drink soon.' And the mare, with some dim remembrance of the tongue that had been familiar to her when she was a foal, whinnied softly, and swung her head to nuzzle at his shoulder. When she was cooled off enough, he brought her a pail of water, and then filled her manger with fresh hay and a handful of beans to keep her happy while he got on with her grooming.

Footsteps came across the yard, loud in the breathless hush, and a shadow darkened the doorway; and he looked up to see Glaucus, cool from the baths and exquisite in a tunic of pale green silk. Beric drew himself to attention, making the obeisance that had become habit with him now.

Glaucus acknowledged it with a friendly nod, and propped himself against the manger. Beric wondered what he had come for. He was often in the stables, but that was to visit the white chariot team that he used as his own, though they were actually his father's. He seemed to be taking an interest in Venetia, watching her eat. ' She is only playing with her food,' he said after a moment. ' Why? '

' She is tired and not hungry,' Beric told him. ' No one could be hungry in such weather as this.' He jerked his head towards the open doorway, beyond which the sunshine was growing dim and sulphurous.

' Take the cloths off a moment, and let's have a look at her.'

Beric did as he was bid, and Glaucus ran an experienced eye over the glossy flanks and beautiful arched neck. ' She has been over hot.'

' I know,' Beric said. ' May I cover her again now? '

' Yes, of course. If she is out of condition——'

' She is not out of condition,' Beric said quickly. ' She has been——'

' Over ridden on a hot day. Yes, I know.' The other sounded friendly, and Beric looked up to encounter a grin and a cocked eyebrow of amused understanding that somehow failed to act on him as it did on most people who came within the range of Glaucus's charm. ' My father is a vile horseman, is he not? '

F

'If he is, it is not for me to say so,' Beric said stiffly. He wondered why the son of the house, who had never before spoken to him save to toss him an order, should come and talk to him like this.

'No. But it is true, none the less. He should never attempt to ride anything less than an elephant—which is what I came to talk to you about.'

'Sir?' Beric gazed at him in bewilderment.

Glaucus drew a hand lightly down Venetia's neck, watching it. 'Yes,' he said reflectively. 'As you say, she is not out of condition, but I think that it would take little to get her out of condition.' He raised his eyes to Beric's face and added, as though changing the subject, 'Have you begun saving to buy your freedom yet?'

'It is not easy to save, without money,' Beric said, after a surprised silence.

'Could you do with a gold aurus to start the fund? Or to have fun with, if that appeals to you better?'

Beric was suddenly on his guard. 'How should I have to earn it?'

'Quite simply. Now listen. There's no one in the hayloft, is there?'

'No.'

'Well then, the thing is that Venetia is wasted on my father, while a friend of mine, a man who rides as she deserves to be ridden, is itching to have her. You can't wonder. She is a beauty, and goes like the wind, don't you, my lady?' He drew his hand again down the mare's neck, while Beric, who knew that she was a beauty and went like the wind, stood warily looking on. 'Well, my father is being as stubborn as a mule about selling her—I wish he was as easy about selling his horses as he is about selling his slaves—but if she was to go suddenly out of condition, *badly* out of condition, he would be only too pleased to sell her, and at half what she is worth, lest he be not able to sell her at all. I know my father. . . . There are—ways, I think, for anyone skilled in horsecraft? Ways which leave no trace and do no lasting harm to the

72

horse? It would have to be done while that old dotard
Hippias is out of the way.'

' Yes, it would have to be done while Hippias is out of the
way,' agreed Beric.

' Well, then? '

' I do not think that I understand.'

The other laughed. ' Don't pretend to be a half-wit.
However, if you would liefer have it in so many words, you
get the mare into poor condition, my father sells her off in a
hurry to this friend of mine, who wants her so badly that he'll
forgive me a whole fistful of money that I owe him, in exchange for having got her, let alone at half what she is worth—
and you have an aurus for your pains.'

' If you need money to pay this debt, why not ask your
father for it? ' Beric said.

Glaucus shrugged, still half laughing. ' My father has
certain economies. Look at the way he buys his own slaves,
and so does Nigellus out of his commission. Certain economies, and I am one of them.'

' The Lady Poppaea your mother, then.' All the household knew how the Lady Poppaea adored and spoiled her son.

' Mother never has any money,' said Glaucus, with
engaging frankness. ' Father pays her bills. He even keeps
her jewels when she is not wearing them.' His pleasant voice
hardened a little. ' I did not come here to be cross-
questioned. Will you do it? '

' No,' Beric said. ' I will not.'

Glaucus was clearly surprised. ' You'll not get more than
an aurus,' he said.

' It is in my heart that I do not want your aurus.'

' Oh, come now.' Glaucus tried another laugh, but it
sounded a little uneasy in the heavy silence of the nearing
storm. ' My father can get another mare, and he will not
miss the money. If he was not so mean, I should not have to
bother with this sort of game. You are not going to pull a
long face and be righteous about it, are you? '

' No.' Beric shook his head. ' It is only that I will not

73

do it.' He was puzzled by his own determination. He owed
no loyalty to Publius Piso. 'If you would cheat your father,
let you do it with your own hands,' he heard himself say.

An odd change came over Glaucus's handsome face. It
seemed to grow sharper and older before the slave's eyes.
'Who are *you* to take that tone with *me*?' he asked softly
'You are a slave. Had you forgotten that? A slave!
There is no right or wrong for a slave, save the will of his
master.'

Beric said levelly, 'But you are not my master.'

Glaucus looked at him a moment in silence, his eyes
narrowed like a cat's before it spits. 'Not yet,' he said, still
more softly. 'No, not yet; but who knows what the fates
hold in store for us?' It was unmistakably a threat. He
thrust off from the manger against which he had been leaning
all this while, and strolled towards the stable door, beyond
which the day had suddenly darkened to the colour of a
bruise; and then turned to face Beric once more. From
somewhere a long way off came a low mutter of thunder
which seemed to intensify rather than break the silence
between them. As it died away, suddenly and most unexpectedly, Glaucus flung back his head and laughed.
'Never look so solemn, you young idiot; I did but seek to test
you; and I am rejoiced to find you so far above reproach.
Take that for your honesty,' and slipping a hand into the
many-folded silken girdle, he tossed a sestercia to Beric's feet,
and lounged out.

But the laughter had not rung true, and Beric, standing
beside Venetia, with the sestercia lying untouched at his feet,
and staring after him, knew that Glaucus was lying, and, what
was far more dangerous, that Glaucus knew he knew. He had
seen behind the pleasant mask of Glaucus and for a moment
made Glaucus see behind it too, and that was the thing of all
others that Glaucus would never forgive.

Again the thunder muttered; nearer this time, and Venetia, who hated thunder, began to snort and shiver.

74

VII

THE DARK DAYS

GLAUCUS did not forgive. There were many small and indefinable ways of making life wretched for a slave, especially a slave who had been born free, and he used them all, with a delicate skill. They did not at first amount to very much, though they added a good deal to Beric's unhappiness; but Beric had an uneasy feeling that the son of the house was merely keeping his hand in until the chance of some bigger hurt came his way.

Presently Hippias hobbled back to his horses and Beric returned to his work in the house. And the house was a busy place in these days, with the wedding so near. There was a ceaseless coming and going of merchants and jewellers and lawyers, and Lucilla's friends were for ever arriving to talk about the wedding and be shown Lucilla's new clothes and jewels, and going away again, chattering together like a flock of many-coloured birds. Nigellus wore a permanently harassed expression, and the cook, who was a Campagnion and excitable, was almost off his head. The Lady Poppaea passed several times a day from purring contentment to tears and tantrums, and the master of the house fussed and fumed so that his usual pink turned to purple, and when he had to go away for a few days unexpectedly, on business, his entire household heaved sighs of relief.

The day after he left, Beric encountered the Lady Lucilla in the shadowed colonnade of the inner court. All afternoon the garden had been full of girls, laughing and chattering, gay in their pretty flower-coloured tunics, playing little idle games with a hollow golden ball engraved with Greek dancers, eating honeyed apricots and admiring the bride's new bracelets. But now they were all gone, and in the cool

75

of the evening the shadowed court seemed very quiet, with only the drowsy crooning of the coral-footed stock-doves to break the stillness. He was surprised to see that although it would soon be dinner-time, the Lady Lucilla had changed into an old tunic and bunched her hair out of the way with a riband.

'Oh Beric,' she said as soon as she saw him, 'now I need not send for you. I am tired of talking about clothes, and I noticed this afternoon that with all this excitement nobody has remembered to pick the figs on the terrace, so I am going to pick them now. Go you and fetch a basket, and come and help me.'

'Yes, my Lady,' Beric touched palm to forehead, and went quickly to do her bidding.

On the way back he met Glaucus, who raised an eyebrow at the sight of the big willow basket he carried, and demanded to know what he did with it.

'It is for figs,' Beric told him. 'The Lady Lucilla has bidden me to help her gather the figs on the terrace.'

'The Lady Lucilla is a great deal too fond of slaves' company,' said Glaucus. 'I must remember to speak to Valarius about it,' and he walked on. Beric looked after him for a moment, with a frown deepening between his eyes, then continued on his way.

He found Lucilla waiting for him by the fig tree which grew against the blank wall of the slaves' quarters, at one end of the terrace, and they set to work, searching for the figs among the cool, many-fingered leaves. For a while they picked in silence, though once or twice Beric caught Lucilla glancing at him sideways, as though she had something she wanted to say and she was not sure how to begin. The silence lasted until he climbed on to the flat coping of the parapet to reach some figs on the topmost branches, and then she said quickly: 'Oh Beric, do be careful! If you slip you will be in the Forum in a score of pieces before you stop rolling!'

'I shall not slip,' Beric said, turning with a hand on a knotted branch to look out and down. Far below him lay the

Forum area, the heart of Rome, with its pillared and porticoed buildings, its triumphal arches and towering statues, all seeming at that distance like some exquisite toy carved from old ivory and peopled with many-coloured atomies; the hills rising from it amethyst-shadowed in the evening light, the Palatine with its palaces, the Capitoline with its temples, the green pomegranate gardens of the Esquiline. ' You might as well be a bird—an eagle, up here,' he said.

'Yes, I expect you might; but oh, please be careful!' Lucilla begged. ' Finish picking those figs and then come down.'

Beric turned his back on Rome, and busied himself with gathering the figs he had come for and passing them down to her. Then he jumped down himself, with the last few still in his hand. ' See, they are the best on the tree,' he said, holding them out to show her.

She took one of them, its sun-warm purple skin splitting to show the pink flesh inside, and began to eat it. ' In nine days I shall be a married woman, and it will be beneath my dignity to eat figs warm off the tree,' she said, a little regretfully.

' Yes, my Lady.' Beric added the rest of the fruit to those in the basket, and looked up again. ' It is in my heart that I hope you will be very happy.'

Lucilla looked at him almost wonderingly, with the half-eaten fig in her hand. ' You said that as though you really cared,' she said. ' So few people do. They are too busy being pleased that Father has arranged such a good match for me.'

Beric began to stutter. ' I—I do care, my Lady. You have been kind to me, and I—would do *anything*, so that you should be happy.'

' I—think I shall be,' said the Lady Lucilla, and suddenly she smiled. ' I like Valarius. I have liked him ever since I can remember, and he likes me; and he is kind and just. And if you like the husband your father chooses for you, and he likes you——' She finished the fig and licked her fingers;

77

and then, as Beric remained silent, she asked: 'How are the marriages made in Britain?'

'Sometimes they are made between our fathers, but usually it is just that when a young man has slain his first wolf, and is free to marry, he looks among the maidens of the Tribe, and when he finds the right one, if she be willing, he goes to her father and asks for the maiden; and unless something stands in the way, there is a feast, and the maiden's father gives the young man his best spear, and he takes the maiden home to his own hut, to be his woman.'

'It sounds nice for the maiden,' said Lucilla, with a half sigh. 'Sometimes it happens so with us, too, but not often. Almost always it is our fathers who choose. And if Father had chosen me a husband of my own age, it might have been someone like Glaucus, who would have been unkind to me because I am not pretty like Claudia and Dometella.'

Beric looked up from adding a last fig to the basket, and their eyes met in quick understanding. So she also had suffered at Glaucus's hands.

'Beric,' Lucilla said suddenly. 'Beric——'

And he knew that he had been right; there was something she wanted to say to him.

'Yes, my Lady?'

'Beric, when I go to Valarius's house, would you like to come with me? Father has given me Aglæa, my nurse, and I think—I am sure—that he would give you to me, if I asked him.'

Beric could not answer at once. To escape from Glaucus, to go with the Lady Lucilla, who treated him as a human being, and be part of her household and Valarius's, who was kind and just and not for ever selling his slaves, it seemed a thing too good to be true.

'Would you like that, Beric?' Lucilla said. 'If you would, I will ask my father when he comes home.'

'Oh my Lady, I would like it—I would!' Beric took the plump sticky hand she held out to him, and bent, and laid it to his forehead.

. . . . .

78

For three days Beric carried his little newly-lit hope with him. It lay down with him at night, and sounded in the first twittering of sparrows under the eaves that woke him each morning. A year ago nothing but the hope of freedom could have meant so much to him; but now freedom had drawn so far away that the hope of a kind master almost sàtisfied his need for hoping.

Towards the evening of the third day the master of the house returned home, with a great deal of shouting and fuss, a great running to and fro of slaves. When it had all died down a little, and Publius Piso had disappeared into the bath-house to soak off the dust of the journey, the household set about the usual preparations for dinner. Presently Beric took freshly filled lamps into the dining-room, for the evenings were beginning to draw in, and though dinner still began in broad daylight, it was growing dusk before the end, and on his way back across the atrium he met the Lady Lucilla. She was just coming in from the colonnade, with her hands full of little thornless yellow roses, and the white kitten, half grown now, weaving and winding around her; and at sight of him she checked, smiling.

' I am going to ask Father after dinner,' she said.

Beric said, ' Yes, my Lady,' suddenly breathless, now that his hopes were so near to their testing time.

' It will be all right,' Lucilla told him. ' I am sure that it will be all right. When Father has had a bath and a good dinner, he will be in a good mood. Always he is like that when he has just got home from a journey. And see, I am going to make him a wreath, as though it were for a feast; and that will help.'

Before Beric's inner eye rose a vision of Publius Piso's round pink face under the wreath of yellow roses slipping, as his wreaths always did, slightly over one ear.

His eyes met the Lady Lucilla's, and he knew that she was seeing the same thing. They began to laugh, and they were still laughing, a few moments later, when Glaucus strolled in, remarking silkily, ' Gossiping with the slaves as usual, I see, Lucilla.'

79

The laughter went from both of them on the instant; Beric drew back, standing rigidly to attention as he waited to be dismissed, and Lucilla turned on her brother with a small defiant flounce. 'I was telling Beric that after dinner I am going to ask father to give him to me.'

Glaucus sank on to a couch piled with gay embroideries, and smiled up to them. 'I had a feeling something of that sort was in the wind. You are too late, my sweet sister; I have just been closeted with our revered father in the bath-house. He is in a most melting mood, and he has given Beric to me.'

There was a stunned silence. Beric, licking his suddenly dry lips, felt as though he had just taken a blow between the eyes; and yet he knew that deep within him, he had expected something like this to happen.

Lucilla was the first to speak. 'I do not believe you,' she said.

'As you please. But it is perfectly true. Ask Father.'

'I shall! And if it is indeed true, I shall beg him to unmake the gift. He does not know—he does not understand——'

'Do,' Glaucus said lightly. 'It will not do you the least good. You know how Father prides himself on being a man of his word.'

'Glaucus,' his sister said. 'Why did you do it? You do not really want Beric.'

'Oh, but I do. I want a charioteer, for one thing, and Beric handles the team well; I watched him bring them back from exercise the other day. Automedan is hopeless with horses, and I am tired of driving myself everywhere, as though I could not afford a charioteer.'

'As though Father could not afford a charioteer, you mean!'

'Very well, as though Father couldn't afford a charioteer.'

'It is funny how people always think that we are so lucky to have you in the family,' Lucilla said, with a quiet, white intensity. 'You were a horrible boy, and you are a horrible man!'

One by one, now that they were useless, the little yellow roses dropped from her hands to the tessellated floor, and the white kitten began to play with them.

Glaucus made her a small mocking bow, then turned to Beric, where he stood among the fallen ruins of his hopes. For a long moment their gaze met and seemed to lock; and again Glaucus's eyes narrowed like a cat's. ' Get back to your work,' he said.

Beric turned, with the accustomed obeisance, and strode away, all but colliding with the Lady Poppaea, who had just come down from her chamber, her evening toilet complete. The heavy scent of jessamine flowers that always floated about her sickened him—he was to hate the scent of jessamine ever after—as he brushed past her without a word.

She squawked like a startled hen; and behind him as he blundered out into the colonnade, he heard her voice upraised. ' Really! He might have knocked me down! I shall tell your father he must get rid of him—he must get rid of him at once! ' And Glaucus's amused reply,' Ah, but he is no longer Father's to get rid of. Father has just given him to me, and I fancy he is not pleased about it.'

.   .   .   .

Long after the other slaves were asleep that night, Beric lay wakeful in his blanket in the long dormitory, staring into the darkness, sick and battered with longing for his own people. His own people, he thought, bitterly; but he had no people. He had thought of the Tribe as his own people, and the Tribe had cast him out; he had thought of the Romans as his own people, and the Romans had made him a slave; a thing to be bought and sold like a chariot pony but with less fellow feeling than most men had for their chariot ponies. He had no people, no belonging place. It had been so little that he had hoped for; only that he might be the Lady Lucilla's slave in a kinder household than this, and get away from Glaucus, whom he hated, and who hated him. And instead, he was become Glaucus's slave. Out of the darkness he seemed to see Glaucus's face with the pleasant mask fallen from it, the eyes narrowing like an angry cat's as they looked at him.

On the next pallet, Hippias began to mutter in his sleep, as he did sometimes, and a new uneasiness was stirred in Beric, on the old groom's account. . . .

All next day, and all the day after, Beric looked out for a chance to speak with the Lady Lucilla alone, but it was not until the third morning that he found it. That morning Glaucus went out early, with Automedan his body-slave in attendance, to meet a friend at the gymnasium, and a little later Beric learned by overhearing the loud complaints of the Lady Poppaea, who it seemed had wanted to speak to her daughter about something, that the Lady Lucilla had gone down to the temple of Sylvan Pan, without asking leave, and taking only Aglæa, her old nurse, with her.

Beric knew the little temple of Sylvan Pan in the vale between the Viminal and the Esquiline. It was a temple that few people visited nowadays, for the gods of Greece and Rome were falling into disuse, and the gods of Egypt and Persia taking their places. Jupiter and Mars and the like were safe, of course, because they were a national habit, and so the people still sacrificed to them even when they no longer believed in them; but the lesser gods were suffering. People had almost forgotten Pan, and the little temple was fading and falling into ill repair, and the garden in which it stood becoming a flowering wilderness. But for some reason, perhaps for that very reason, the Lady Lucilla liked it, and would sometimes slip down there to talk to the one old saffron-robed attendant priest, and put a sestercia in his bowl, and watch the goldcrests that nested in the osiers and overgrown arbutus of the garden. Beric had been her escort on several such visits, for though the place was quite near her home, it was also near to the Suburra, the teeming slums of Rome, that thrust up the vale towards it in a long tongue, and so she was not really supposed to go unattended.

Hearing that she had gone there now, Beric knew that he would never get a better chance of speaking with her alone, in the few days that were left before her wedding; and laying down Glaucus's fine leather tunic, which he was supposed to

be cleaning, he set out there and then. He would have to
think of an excuse to get him out, for though the gates stood
open, slaves going out had to give their reasons to Agathos
the porter; his brain felt woolly with lack of sleep, so that it
was hard to think at all, but as he crossed the inner court, he
saw a cyclamen-coloured cloak of the Lady Lucilla's flung
across the marble bench. A year of the arm-ring had taught
Beric a certain amount of guile, and he caught up the cloak
in passing, and reached the gate carrying it.

'My Lady has forgotten her mantle,' he told Agathos, 'and
the wind is cold to-day.' And without waiting for Agathos to
point out that there was not a breath of wind stirring, he
strode out into the road. He went down by a narrow back
way that zig-zagged among the high walls of houses, until he
reached the arched entrance to the temple garden, and turned
in under low-hanging scented branches of lemon and myrtle
and arbutus. He found the Lady Lucilla almost at once. She
was sitting on a bench of weathered marble close beside the
temple itself, sitting perfectly still, her head bent to watch a
lizard, green as a living emerald, basking spread-fingered on
the sun-hot stones at her feet; while Aglæa stood just behind
her, her magenta veil making a patch of crude colour against
the faded frieze of nymphs and satyrs.

She looked up quickly as Beric drew near, startling the
lizard, so that it darted off like a flicker of green flame.
'Why, Beric——' she began: then she turned to the other
woman, holding out something in her hand. 'Aglæa, do you
go to the priest, and give him this from me, and ask him to
remember me when he makes the harvest offering.'

There was a chink as the money changed hands, and then
her nurse scuttled off towards the glint of a saffron robe which
showed afar off, where the old attendant priest was busy among
his overgrown lemon trees. The Lady Lucilla turned back
to Beric. 'Is it that you want me to ask Father again? It
would not be any use, Beric. I have tried, but it is as Glaucus
says. Father takes such a dreadful pride in being a man of
his word.'

84

Beric shook his head. 'It is not for myself, my Lady, I—
I——'

'You what?' asked Lucilla, after an unhappy pause.

'My Lady, I had to come, to ask you if you would ask your
father to give you Hippias instead of me.'

She looked at him in bewilderment. 'Hippias? But
Beric, I don't want Hippias, and Valarius has all the stable
slaves he needs.'

Beric came a step nearer in his eagerness. 'Please, my
Lady! Hippias is getting old; he's getting past hard work
since he broke his leg, but he is a master with horses! No
stable could be the worse for having him in it. Only if you
leave him here, I think—I am afraid—you see, he is my friend,
the only friend I have in the household, and your brother
——' He could not go on. The fear that had come to him
in the night seemed so fantastic now in the daylight.

But the Lady Lucilla seemed to find nothing fantastic in
it. 'You are afraid that Glaucus may try to hurt you by
hurting him?'

Beric gulped. 'It—— Oh, I know it is craziness to think
such a thing; I am of too little account in his eyes for him
to trouble himself; but it would be so easily done, to put
the idea into the master's head that he needs a younger
groom. Hippias is so afraid of being sold. He was very
afraid when he broke his leg.'

'Did he tell you to ask me?'

Again Beric shook his head. 'No, oh no. It was just my
own idea. I am sorry if it was not a good one.'

The Lady Lucilla got up. 'But it was a very good one,'
she said. 'I will ask Father for Hippias to-night, and if he
gives him to me, nobody shall sell him again; I promise you
that.'

'Thank you, my Lady.' Beric took the two hands she held
out to him, and so realized that he was still carrying her cloak
across his arm. 'My Lady, your mantle. I brought it as an
excuse to come here after you. Will you take it?'

'Give it to me. There. Now you must go back quickly.'

85

Beric hesitated. ' You should not be here alone, my Lady.'

' I am not alone. I have Aglæa and the priest yonder. Besides, no one ever comes here, save sometimes a farmer or herdsman in Rome for the day.' She glanced round her at the over-grown garden. ' That shows plainly enough, too.'

' Not worshippers, no,' Beric insisted. ' But the Suburra is very near.'

' It will not invade this place. Do you know, the old priest told me once that even at night, when all the odd corners of Rome are filled with beggars and cutpurses and poor homeless people, no one comes here, and even the Watch only pokes its nose in at the gate once in the night, and then goes on. He says that people no longer believe in Sylvan Pan when it is the time for offerings, but they are still afraid to catch the smell of goat, here in his garden.' Her voice, which had sunk very low, became practical again. ' You must go now. It is better that Glaucus should not know we have been together, not until after I have asked Father, so you must be back before he is.'

And that was true. Beric touched palm to forehead, and turning, went quickly back the way he had come.

Three days later he stood among the slaves who crowded the doorways of the guest-filled atrium, to see the Lady Lucilla brought down in all the glory of her bridal tunic, crowned with myrtle and rosemary and with her flame-coloured veil drawn close around her, to be married.

Valarius and his friends arrived, and the ceremony began. There was the sharp-sweet smoke of incense rising in blue spirals from the altars of the household gods, and vows taken, and offerings made of corn and wine and milk; and the Lady Lucilla moving through it all, looking small and rather forlorn in her wedding finery.

Was it well with her? Beric wondered, craning his neck to glimpse her little dumpy figure beside the tall, set, soldierly one of Valarius. But when the ceremony was over, and they turned together to face the throng, and Lucilla put back her flame-coloured veil, somehow he was reassured, not by anything in her face, for she looked white and scared, but by the way Valarius took her hand and looked down at her. All would be well with the Lady Lucilla.

When the feasting that followed the ceremony was over and the dusk came, the guests, many of them holding torches, gathered in the outer courtyard; and the bride was led out to them, carrying three denarii in her hand, one for her husband, and one for the gods of her new household, and one for the gods of the nearest crossroads. Two of the girls who had been with her most often in the garden followed her, carrying her spindle and distaff; and Valarius and his friends closed round her, and swept her out through the gates and away into her new life. Many of the guests streamed after them, and right at the tail of the procession, with Aglæa, who carried the white kitten, walked old Hippias, still bewildered as to why he was going with the Lady Lucilla at all, and more than a little sad at leaving his own horses, but unutterably relieved to be going to a master who did not sell off his slaves when they grew old.

And standing in the shadows with the other slaves, Beric watched the little gay torchlit procession winding out through the gateway, carrying with it the only two friends he had in the world.

VIII

BREAKING-POINT

'I HAVE decided to change your name,' Glaucus said, on the day after the wedding, lounging at ease on his sleeping-couch, while Beric stood before him. 'From now on, you will be called Hyacinthus.'

So even his name was to be taken from him, the one thing he had left, the thing that made him himself and nobody else. He had a sudden feeling of panic, as though the last fragile thread that still linked him to the life he knew was being snapped by the slender, ruthless hands of his new master. 'My name is Beric,' he said stubbornly.

'Beric is not a name, it is a mere sound; good enough, doubtless, for the savages who called you by it, but not good enough for me,' Glaucus said, almost idly, as though it were a fact so obvious as to be scarcely worth mentioning. 'From now on, your name is Hyacinthus. You understand?'

'I—understand.'

'Oh, and another thing, while I remember it. I will not have you hanging round the stables. Now that my father has bought a decent slave in place of that old dotard Hippias, they have no need of your help with the horses. You are not to go into the stables at all, unless by my orders to bring round the chariot. The care of the team is no longer any concern of yours.'

'It is always better that a team should know the man who drives them,' Beric said urgently.

'Doubtless that is the barbarian way, but it is not mine. You have your orders, and if you forget them, I will have you whipped to help you remember another time. Now get out.'

Beric turned on his heel without a word, and also without

the usual obeisance. It was a very futile gesture of defiance, he realized that, even as he made it. And almost in the same instant there was a quick movement behind him as Glaucus sprang from the couch, and he was caught by the shoulders and spun round to face his master. 'Have you not forgotten something?' Glaucus said softly, his fingers biting into Beric's shoulders. Beric remained silent. 'You should not leave my presence without saluting, because you are a slave, and I am your master; because you belong to me as my sandals belong to me. That is another thing for you to remember.'

Beric stood there tense and rigid under the gripping hands. If he had been a dog, the hackles would have risen on his neck; and something of that must have shown in his face, for Glaucus said quickly: 'Do not you dare to show your teeth to me, you barbarian wolf's whelp!' and withdrawing one hand, struck him a sharp, deliberate blow across the cheek. 'Now go, Hyacinthus.'

For an instant longer Beric stood perfectly still, with the deepening marks of four fingers burning in his cheek. Then he made his obeisance, and, almost choking, turned and strode out.

He was Hyacinthus, Glaucus's slave, and without hope.

The months that followed were evil ones for Beric, a black time of injustice and casual-seeming cruelties and humiliations that made him writhe. Friendless in the great household, forbidden even the company of the horses, without any hope for the future, he got somehow through day after dreary day. Occasionally Lucilla came to visit her mother, but he seldom caught more than a distant glimpse of her. Glaucus saw to that.

Publius Piso said he had been right, after all. That slave *was* sullen. A good worker, doubtless, a fine charioteer, but sullen. He was never mistaken.

So things dragged on until the evening when Publius Piso gave a dinner-party to celebrate his election as one of the city's four Ædiles for the coming year.

It was a big dinner-party, and Beric had been brought in to swell the number of the table slaves, as had happened more

89

than once before. Earlier that evening he had paraded with
the rest for Nigellus's inspection, all in new tunics issued for the
occasion, and now, with the first course of eggs and anchovies
and sharp-tasting herbs already on the table, he stood
against the frescoed wall and looked about him. The whole
scene seemed to swim in honey-coloured light that fell from
the high silver wall lamps and fountained upwards from those
on the polished citron-wood table. Cedar logs were burning
on the charcoal in the braziers, the scent of them mingling
like incense with that of the flowers on the table: winter
cyclamen and anemones and aromatic sprigs of rosemary
scattered among the gleaming dishes and banked around the
silver figures of the household gods. The guests reclining on
the softly cushioned dining-couches were each wearing a
flower wreath, too, in which, if the laughter had not been
quenched in him long ago, Beric would have thought that
most of them looked distinctly comic. His gaze wandered
over the faces of the guests, all turned towards their host as he
poured the first oblation to the household gods. They were
all men (even the Lady Poppaea had been banished to dine
in her own chamber), mostly fellow-magistrates of Publius
Piso's. Valarius should have been there, of course, but he
had had to go south on business. Glaucus, the only young
one there, and the only one whose wreath somehow did not
look ridiculous, was behaving beautifully in his part of a boy
among his elders, turning from one to another with just the
right touch of deference that made them feel senior without
making them feel old.

How well he did it, Beric thought, watching him from his
place against the wall, with the quiet, long-biding hatred of
his foster people.

But to-night Beric's chief attention, which until now had
been focused upon his master in whatever company they might
be, as though by the very strength of the hatred between them,
was gradually caught and held by someone else: by a man
with the distinctive carriage of the regular soldier, placed
directly across the table from the son of the house, and deep

in quiet talk with an elderly senator beside him. This, Beric knew, for he had seen the man before, though never at close quarters, was Titus Drusus Justinius, a Senior Centurion of the Legions and a noted builder of roads and drainer of marshes to the outermost ends of the Empire. But it was something about the man himself, and not his reputation, that caught at the awareness of the slave against the wall, and indeed he was a figure to stand out in any company: a squat, barrel-chested man with immensely powerful shoulders, and arms whose length made him appear grotesque when one saw him standing. His dark, lean-cut face, with the great hooked nose and the black brows that almost met below the brand of Mithras on the forehead, might well have been a desert Arab's, but when he raised his eyes from the wine-cup in his hand, instead of being, as one expected them to be black with the sun behind them—they were the cold quiet grey of northern seas; the eyes of a man who might be merciless at times, but would never be unjust. It would be good to serve a man like that. ' If I were his slave! ' Beric thought. ' If only I were his slave! '

He found that the sharp hunger-making first course was over, and it was time to carry round the bowls of scented water, and soft linen towels for the guests to wash their fingers. The next course was brought in: giant turbot on dishes as broad as bucklers, kid boiled in milk with sweet herbs, roast flamingo coming to table in all their white-and-scarlet plumage. Crito, the head table slave, carved before his master, and for a while Beric and his fellows were kept busy carrying plates and dishes and keeping the wine-cups filled with red Falernian or golden Greek wine.

By the time the second course also was done with, the mood of the company, which had been somewhat reserved at first— Publius Piso's dinner-parties were apt to have a faint frost on them—had warmed into cheerfulness. There was a general air of ungirding. Voices grew louder and eyes brighter; men began to laugh with each other, and their banquet wreaths slipped a little sideways.

91

'To our new Ædile,' somebody called out, holding up a freshly charged wine-cup. 'Success to him, and may he have cause to give other celebration dinners, as good as this one, to his admiring friends!'

All round the table, cups were raised. 'To the new Ædile!' echoed from all sides, and Publius Piso was in his element as he bowed and beamed his acknowledgement, swelling and blossoming in the warmth of their friendly laughter.

The main business of dinner was over now, and Beric and his fellows had removed the empty chargers and set in their places dishes of little sweet cakes and silver baskets filled with honeyed apricots and green and purple bran-stored grapes. And Beric, standing watchful in his place, heard the laughter and the cheerful raillery rising all round him.

'Four years from now.' A little merry man cocked an eye like a blackbird's towards his host. 'That will be the day, eh, Publius?'

'Publius Piso for Consul!' someone joined in from the foot of the table.

'Vote for Piso. More Games and fewer taxes!' chanted a third, and there was a general laugh.

'I'll vote for you, if you will ask me to dinner again and give me some more of this vintage!' promised the man with an eye like a blackbird.

Publius Piso looked down his nose, pleased, but at the same time slightly disapproving of so much levity on a serious subject. 'If, when the time comes, my fellow-citizens should do me the supreme honour to elect me to the Consulship,' he said, 'I trust, my friends, that you will each and every one of you give me the happiness—the very great happiness—of seeing you at my poor table on the third evening after my election.'

'Accepted! accepted!' cried the guests, and a man with a wreath of white cyclamen slipping over a bottle nose avowed with profound dignity, 'Speaking as I trust I may for the whole of this assembled company—though come to think of it

I can't see why I should—I say that failing the—er—in short, the shears of Atropos, we will each and every one of us be here upon that er—auspicious occasion. Each and every one of us. After you with the almond cakes, Clodias.'

'Not quite every one of us,' said the old senator quietly. 'There will, I think, be one member of our gathering here to-night who will be otherwise engaged, and at rather too great a distance from Rome.' And he glanced at the Centurion beside him.

Other eyes were turned in the same direction. 'Percol! I thought you were done with the outposts of Empire,' said the bird-eyed man.

'Did you?' said the Centurion tranquilly, speaking almost for the first time to the company in general.

'Where is it to be this time?'

'Still Britain,' said the Centurion. 'Still my same marsh and my old job.'

The quietly spoken words seemed to leap out at Beric as a shout, and his gaze, which had been on his master, whipped back to the Centurion with a startled intensity.

'When do you return?' someone asked.

'I sail from Ostia on the third day from now.'

A buzz of interest had broken out all round the table. 'I had not realized that you were going north again,' said a man at the foot of the table, reaching for a honeyed apricot. 'Surely you are due for promotion?'

'I am.'

They looked at him, puzzled, and Glaucus burst out: 'But, sir, do you mean that you are going to let that slip for the sake of—of a few yokelands of *marsh*?' He checked with a show of half-laughing dismay. 'Oh forgive me, sir; I had no business to say that.'

Centurion Justinius made a small gesture, as though dismissing the apology. 'I mean precisely that,' he said. 'I have very few leanings towards the work of a camp commandant, even fewer towards the Prætorian Guard and life one long ceremonial parade. I have the gravest doubts of

my abilities as a Præfect, but I am a thoroughly good engineer.'
He glanced round the table, and his voice lost the faintly
mocking note that had been in it until now. 'I have had the
draining of this marsh from the outset; from the first survey,
four years ago. It is the last marsh that I shall reclaim, and I
had lief see the thing completed, before my time comes to take
my wooden foil and bid good-bye to the Eagles.'

'I believe your marshes and your roads are more to you
than flesh and blood!' said Publius Piso, almost fretfully.

'Wife and son at the very least,' said the bird-eyed man,
with a laugh. 'A marsh for a wife and a straight paved road
for a son; your born engineer needs no other.'

The Centurion was gently swirling the wine in his cup, and
watching the swing of it. There was an odd half-smile on his
mouth, but he said nothing.

'Then we shall be seeing no more of you until this marsh
of yours is finally safe from the sea?' someone broke the small
silence.

Justinius set down his wine-cup with delicate precision, and
raised those bleak grey eyes of his. 'I very much doubt, my
dear Fulvius, if you will see anything more of me even then. I
have a feeling that I shall strike my roots in the north. My
mother was part British, after all.'

They stared at him blankly. 'Zeus!' said his host, and
then added hastily: 'Well, well. Durinum is a pleasant
place to retire to, so I have heard—or Aquæ Sulis.'

The Centurion shook his head. 'Very pleasant, I believe,
but not for me. When first I went out, I took over a derelict
farmstead on the high fringe of the marsh, and put in an old
Optio of mine and his wife to look after it. At the outset
I only meant to use it for winter quarters while the job lasted,
but I have grown to feel the place my home. Servius has
already wrought wonders, and presently, when we have
finished clearing the scrub, and brought the land back into
good heart, we shall run a few horses on it. That is a good
way to retire—better than drinking the waters at Aquæ
Sulis.'

'You are not afraid that the time may come when you will
feel the pull of civilization?' said the old Senator gently.

'No. I have enjoyed my leave in Rome, but I have lived
over long in the wilds to settle into the life of cities. Civilization is too tight a fit for me now, so that I find it hard to
breathe.' His harsh face softened a little. 'I want my wide
marsh skies, and my small outland farm, and the wild geese
flighting down from the north with the autumn gales.'

His words struck home to the young slave standing against
the wall. 'I also, my own skies—my own hills!' he could
have cried it out; for a moment the crowded, lamp-lit room
lost reality, and he was a thousand miles and two long years
away, and free. Only for a moment, and then the room
clamped down on him again, and he became aware that
Glaucus, now very flushed and bright of eye, had just set
down his wine-cup empty, and was crooking an impatient
finger for a slave to refill it.

Automedan, who had also been pressed into service, was
pouring for someone else at the moment, and Beric was nearest
to his master. He stepped forward, and bent to fill the cup
which the other held, from the slender jug of Falernian in his
hand.

He had been trained to pour from a distance, so that the
wine fell curving in a slender stream into the cup below; but
as he tipped the jug, a slight, abrupt movement caught at the
tail of his eye, and his glance flicked up for an instant—to meet
the eyes of the Centurion, fixed on his face with a startled intensity, an eager searching look, that was almost painful. For
the merest breath of time their gaze met, so strongly that it was
like an actual touch, before Beric's flicked down again to the
wine-cup in his master's hand, but the mischief was done.
His hand, checking at the wrong instant, had broken the
perfect arc of the falling wine, so that it spattered a few drops,
bright as blood, on to Glaucus's wrist, and up across the jewel-
clasped sleeve of his tunic.

Glaucus broke off midway in some remark to his neighbour,
and with a sharp exclamation of annoyance, glanced up to see

95

who the clumsy slave might be, and seeing—struck him full in the face.

It was not a particularly hard blow, and certainly it was not the first that his slave had had from him, but the heavy signet ring which he wore cut Beric's mouth, and at the taste of blood between his teeth, salt and sweet together, some hard-held control snapped in him. Perhaps it was because of that moment, scarcely passed, when his freedom and his own world had returned to him so vividly. . . . Suddenly he could bear no more.

He was not conscious of shifting his grip on the wine-jug and dashing the whole contents into the handsome, hated face before him. He did not realize that he had done it, until he saw Glaucus gasping, with the red Falernian trickling off his chin and the crimson stain of it spreading over his breast and shoulders.

The sudden hush seemed to become a bubble of utter stillness, swelling and swelling, until it burst, and uproar rushed in from all sides, as Publius Piso let out a bellow of fury, and the outraged guests shot up on their couches, and Beric's fellow-slaves flung themselves upon him as upon a dog suddenly gone wild. Within a few moments it was all over and he had been dragged back and was standing helpless in the grip of many hands, his arms twisted behind him.

The uproar ended as swiftly as it had begun. Only Publius Piso, damson-coloured with fury, his wreath of violets slipping wildly over one eye, was spluttering out barely intelligible exclamations, orders to his slaves, and apologies, that seemed to be as much for his son's disgraceful behaviour as anything else, to his guests. Glaucus shook himself clear of the slaves who had sprung to mop him down and turned to look at Beric, where he stood panting in the grip of his captors. Once again his eyes narrowed like those of a cat before it spits.

'You must be mad,' he said very softly. 'That is the kindest thing to think about you. There is only one place for a mad slave, and that is the salt-mines. We must arrange for you to go there, Hyacinthus.'

Distaste showed on the faces of the guests; one or two of them shrugged, and glanced at each other with raised brows, but only one cut across the laws of custom and good manners to speak out in defence of the wretched slave, and that was Justinius, who had grown unused to the ways of civilization.

'Don't be a fool, Glaucus; it was my doing that he spilled the wine in the first place, for I moved quickly and the movement caught his eye. There was no just cause for a blow, and if you are in the habit of striking without cause, you should not be surprised if the blows rebound.'

'And must we all freeze, like so many deer who scent danger, every time a slave pours wine, lest we distract his attention?' Glaucus flung back at his father's guest, and then, belatedly recovering his manners, added more quietly: 'I beg your forgiveness, sir, but I know this particular slave and his deserts.' His narrowed, glittering gaze lingered on Beric's face, moved to the slaves who held him, and back again. 'Thirty strokes, I think, for a mad dog. That can wait until the morning, however. It will be something for him to look forward to, through the night. Take him away and chain him up, lest he bite somebody.'

IX

ESCAPE!

ERIC was hustled from the room and along familiar colonnades and corridors, and thrust at last down several steps into a small disused storeroom below ground level. It was ice cold, and quite empty in the light of a torch somebody had brought in after him, save for a jumble of derelict gardening tools and such like, stacked in a corner. He made no resistance when he was thrust over to a big staple projecting from the rough tufa wall—the place had been used as a makeshift prison before—nor when somebody brought an iron shackle with a strong though slender chain attached to it, and snapped it on to his wrist. They padlocked the other end of the chain through the staple; then they thronged out, taking the lamp with them, and the door swung to behind them, and he heard the heavy key turn in the lock. A needless precaution, he thought dully.

But almost at once the key turned again, and the door opened, and Nigellus appeared in the opening, with a distant light behind him. 'Here—you will want a cloak,' he said, not unkindly, and tossed something towards Beric that fell in heavy folds across his feet. Then he shut the door again, and relocked it, and again Beric was left standing in the dark.

He made no move to pick up the cloak, no move at all, for a long time. He was completely dazed. Then, very slowly and painfully, the power to think returned to his numbed brain, like feeling returning to a numbed limb, and he began to realize what had happened, and what was going to happen. Still standing, staring straight before him into darkness that was like a black pad over his eyes, he thought about what was going to happen; not the scourging that he was to suffer in the morning, but the horror that loomed beyond that. The salt-mines. It had been no idle threat of Glaucus's; he knew that all too surely. A man sent to the salt-mines might take years to die, but his toes and fingers dropped off first, much as though he were a leper, and he usually went mad.

His brain was still working slowly and confusedly, but one thought leapt up clear out of the confusion. Escape! Whatever he did now, nothing that happened to him could be worse than the salt-mines. He had nothing to lose. The old reasons that had kept him from attempting to escape before, as they kept so many of his kind, returned to him, but he put them away. No use, yet, to think of what he was to do afterwards. The first thing was to get out. To get out!

Turning his head, he could make out the paler square of the small window high in the wall. It was a very small window, but he reckoned that if he could get free of the staple to which he was chained he might be able to wriggle through it. He put back a hand in the dark, found the staple, and shook it experimentally. It felt hopelessly firm, as though one would have to pull down the whole wall to get it out; but it was his one hope, since there would obviously be no breaking the chain. He twisted his hands in the chain, and wedged his feet against the wall, and heaved back, straining with every muscle he possessed, shifted a little, and tried again, tried until the sweat pricked out on him and his heart was drubbing against his ribs, and his hands were cut and bleeding. But the staple was as firm as ever.

He must have a tool of some sort, something to act as a lever. Maybe there was something in the pile of rubbish in the corner, if only he could reach it. Straining to the full length of his chain, he tried to reach it with his free hand. No good. He crouched down, and going all out along the floor, felt about with one outstretched foot. His toes found something in the dark, and he hooked it towards him. Various bits of the pile collapsed with a crash that sounded to him like the whole of Rome falling; and for a long moment he lay rigid with his breath caught in his throat, listening for any sound of raised voices or hurrying feet. But the walls of the storeroom were thick, and it seemed that no hint of the clatter had reached the outer world. He pulled towards him the clutter of objects that had fallen on his foot, and found among them a broken pruning-hook with which he was able to catch and drag more of the pile towards him. Almost at once he found what he wanted: the remains of an iron rake used for tending the hypercaust fires. The head of it was badly corroded, but the lower end of the shaft was sound enough. Catching it up, he turned back with it to the staple, hesitated, and then, laying it down, felt about for the broken pruning-hook, and with the jagged end of it began to scrape and dig at the mortar in which the staple was bedded.

It was old mortar, and almost at once he felt the tool bite, and heard the soft rustle of falling mortar dust, then a spatter as some larger fragments broke away. He worked on steadily; there was an odd calm on him, and he felt no frantic haste. Presently, having done all he could with the pruning-hook, he laid it by, and taking up the iron rake, dropped a finger-length of the shaft down through the staple, and began to use his lever. For what seemed an eternity he fought the thing as though it were a living enemy. He was streaming with sweat, sobbing for breath, deaf with the drumming of his own heart, when at last there was a crack, and a grating sound followed by a sharp rattle of falling plaster, and the staple came out into his hands.

For a few moments he stood gasping, straining to listen for outside sounds through the surge of the blood in his ears. Then carefully and deliberately he slipped the staple free of his chain and laid it down with the iron rake, wound the chain round his shackled wrist, taking the padlock into the palm of his hand, and began to feel about for the cloak which Nigellus had brought him, and which he had kicked into a corner. He found it at last, and crossing to the high window, reached up and bundled it through, hearing it slither softly on to the pavement outside. Then he got his hands on to the stone sill to draw himself up. It was not easy; he had to let go the padlock before he could get a grip with his left hand, and heard it ring and rasp against the stone as he dragged himself up. The window was very small—so small that if he had been a year or two older he would not have been able to get through at all; but although he was as tall as he would ever be, his shoulders had not yet fully broadened into a man's, and he was as supple as an otter. Even so, it was a horribly tight fit. But he managed it somehow, and once his shoulders were through, the rest was easy enough, for the window, which was so high above the storeroom floor, was almost on ground level on the outside, and he had only to pull himself forward on his hands, across the tumbled cloak lying there. He drew his legs out after him, and stood up. He was in the narrow slipway that ran from the slaves' quarters to the outer court.

He stooped for the cloak and flung it round his shoulders, suddenly aware that the touch of the February night was icy on his skin through his sweat-soaked tunic; and had just started down the slipway, when a gleam of torchlight and the sound of voices beyond the mouth of it sent him flattening back against the wall, frozen like a wild thing that smells the hunter. Clearly, the disturbed dinner-party had been patched up, and the guests were only now leaving. Praying that the light would not reach him, praying that no one would pass this way from the slaves' quarters, he waited while the torches came and went and voices and footsteps crossed the court. Someone made a joke, and someone laughed, and the laughter sounded very loud and near. But at last the outer court was dark and silent again. Beric waited while he counted fifty, after the last reflection of the torchlight died from the wall opposite, but he dared wait no longer, for at any moment a slave might come this way as the shortest cut to his bed. He darted down to the alley-mouth, paused an instant, listening, and then walked boldly across. The bolder the better, for anyone catching sight of him would be the less likely to suspect anything.

He had always known that the outer court was a wide one, but to-night it seemed to stretch out like a vast plain in a nightmare, and when he came to the middle of it, it was all

that he could do not to break into a run. He reached the far
side at last, slipped between two buildings, turned a corner,
mounted a couple of shallow steps, and an instant later was
crouching under a dense mass of ilex and oleander in the
garden. There he waited, watching and listening from his
cold cover, until the lamps were quenched in the colonnade,
and then in the rooms beyond; until at last all was quiet, and
the great house slept, save for Priscus the watchman, who
would not sleep all night, except perhaps a little, between his
rounds. Beric got up, stiff and half frozen, and stole out to
the shed where the garden and odd-job tools were kept.

He got the door open without a sound, and slipped inside,
but it was no easy task to find what he wanted in the dark, and
every moment he was terrified of bringing down a fall of tools
which would wake the household and fetch Priscus with his
lantern and his cudgel on to the scene. At last his delicately
questing fingers found what he wanted—a heavy file—and
carrying it, he slipped out, closed the door with agonising
care behind him, and set off for the terrace at the foot of the
garden.

He climbed on to the parapet just beside the fig tree whose
fruit he and Lucilla had gathered last summer. It was leaf-
less now, gaunt and twisted against the star-powdered sky, as
he looked upward; but he could see the little dark blobs that
were next summer's figs, and already, on the branch under his
hand, he could feel the promise of the thickening leaf-buds.
Far below him a few lights still burned like scattered jewels in
the black bowl of the hills.

' Be careful! ' Lucilla had said. ' If you slip you will be
in the Forum in a score of pieces before you stop rolling.'
But that would be better than the salt-mines. He dropped
over, found a narrow foothold at the base of the wall, and a
few moments later had reached the corner and was scrambling
up the few feet of rocky turf that rose almost sheer behind the
slaves' bath-house. He came to another wall, swung himself
over, and was standing in a narrow gap between the Piso
house and its neighbour. He gained the street, and crossing

it, dived into the familiar track that sniped downhill between the walls of other houses.

His most pressing need now was a quiet place where he could rid himself of his shackle without fear of interruption, and instinctively he turned to the one such place that he knew of in all Rome. 'No one comes here; even the Watch only pokes its nose in at the gate once a night, and then goes on,' Lucilla had said. He came to the crumbling archway, and turned in under the low-hanging branches of lemon and arbutus. The garden of Sylvan Pan seemed less friendly in the starlight, more remote. The temple looked almost a ruin—the ruin of a temple in a lost world. The gloom under the tangled masses of ilex and lemon and oleander seemed darker and more mysterious than the shadows in the Piso garden had done, and for an instant, as he went forward, fear brushed him by, rustling like a night wind through the grass— not the fear of discovery, but of something that he could give no name to, beautiful and terrible, and smelling of goat. 'He says that people have forgotten Sylvan Pan when it is the time for offerings, but they still fear to catch the smell of goat, here in his garden.'

The thing passed almost before it came, and Beric went on, making for the part of the garden farthest from the cell where the old attendant priest lived. And there, in the black shadows under a tangled mass of evergreens, he settled down with the stolen file. It was maddeningly slow work, and at any moment Glaucus might be going down to gloat over his prisoner, and find him gone. A score of times Beric was on the edge of catching up his file and running while the way was still open, with the shackle still on his wrist, but he could not get out of Rome except by one of the gates, and at the gates there was always the chance of being searched. So, setting his teeth, he went on patiently driving the file back and forth along the scratch that gradually widened and deepened to a furrow on the surface of his shackle; pausing sometimes to feel how the furrow was getting on, and then returning to the ceaseless movement, to and fro, to and fro.

Once the fear came back, whispering with the night wind through the ilex leaves, and left him shivering as it passed on; once he thought he caught the distant notes of a shepherd's pipe, but when he checked the rasp of his file to listen with a thumping heart and prickling skin, all he could hear above the distant surf-roar of the city was a bird calling across the valley from the pomegranate gardens of the Esquiline.

He had been maybe an hour at his task, maybe two, when the mailed footsteps of the Watch patrol came ringing down the lane; and he froze under the evergreens, as they halted at the gateway, and peering through the leaves saw the glint of the lantern light on steel caps and corselets. But after a few moments there was a sharp order, and the lantern flickered out of sight, and he heard the mailed footsteps ringing away down the lane. The Lady Lucilla had been right.

With a gasp of relief, Beric set to work again. And not long after, the file broke through the last filament of metal, and he was able to force the shackle open and drag it from his wrist. Now for the silver arm-ring that marked him for a slave of the Piso house. It had been tight enough over his elbow on the night that Nigellus had issued it to him, and his arm had thickened since then, but by spitting on his hand and smearing the spittle again and again over the thickest part of his elbow, to make it slippery, he got it off eventually.

Now at last he could go! He thrust the file into the soft earth, having no further use for it, and got up. Again, as he went back through the garden to the gate, he seemed to catch the faint piping under the leaves; but again, as he checked to listen, it was gone. He checked once more, to break a switch of rosemary from a bush by the gate. Then he was out in the narrow lane, out in the world of men again.

He turned back the way he had come, twisting shackle and arm-ring together by the slender chain as he went, twisting the switch of rosemary in and out around them both; and crossing the ridge of the Viminal and the vale beyond came up by many winding streets on to the brow of the Pincian. He knew which of the houses there was Valarius's, although he had never been inside it, and before the portico he checked, looking up at the dark mass of buildings surrounding the forecourt. Somewhere in there the Lady Lucilla would be asleep. He stood for a little while considering, then, tearing a strip from his already ragged cloak, he muffled the shackle and arm-ring in it, and went into the portico. There was a space between the top of the gate and the arched lintel, and taking careful aim, he tossed the bundle, and heard it fall with a thud and a faint jangle on the other side. Then he turned away from the sleeping house.

In the morning someone would find them, the filed shackle and the Piso arm-ring, twisted together with a switch of rosemary, and bring them to Valarius. No, he was away. To the Lady Lucilla herself; and at first she would be puzzled. But when she heard what had happened, she would understand, and know that he had come here in the dark, and left them for her, because he had no other means of saying good-bye to her.

He took the next street that led downhill and came out at last into the Flaminian Way, the great road that led from the Forum out through the Flaminian Gate, north-east two hundred miles and more, to Rimini.

The Flaminian Way was as crowded and more noisy now in the darkest hour of the night even than it was by day, for though there were fewer people about on foot, and most of the shops were shut, and the litters and chariots of the great folk lacking, the heavy wheeled traffic that was not allowed in the streets of Rome in the daytime was rumbling up and down. There were endless streams of market carts coming and going; great wagons toiling up from the Tiber side, cattle being driven in for slaughter. In one place, as Beric went by, a huge dray, piled with blocks of yellow Lydian marble and drawn by several file of oxen, had got a wheel jammed in a rut, and was holding up the traffic of three streets, while a sweating and swearing knot of men struggled by the light of a couple of lanterns to get it out.

The Flaminian Gate seemed mercilessly bright with lanterns

and torches when he reached it, and the crowds that had been shifting shadows before sprang into sharp-edged reality as they reached it. Beric hesitated for a short while in the deep gloom of a doorway, watching the outgoing stream of traffic, telling himself that even if he *were* searched, as sometimes happened at the gate, there was nothing to betray him—unless the fine new tunic under such a threadbare cloak struck anyone as odd, or his indoor sandals seemed suspicious, unless the slave-ring had left a suggestive mark on his arm : unless his cut lip and torn hands and the bruises on him had any kind of tale to tell—unless—unless—— He felt as though ' Runaway Slave ' were branded on his forehead for all to see. But it was no good standing here until the sun rose and his escape was discovered.

He nerved himself as for a cold plunge, and praying to every god that he had ever heard of, from Sylvan Pan to Lugh of the Shining Spear, thrust off into the stream, just behind a respectable-looking old man leading a donkey whose empty panniers had doubtless been full of vegetables for the market. Nearer and nearer loomed the gate; he was in the full harsh glare of the torchlight now. He walked steadily, keeping very close to the old man, so that the guards, who would have seen him and his donkey many times before, might think that they were together.

Now the torchlit arch was right overhead, and his feet rang hollow in the enclosed space; three more steps—two—one. Out of the tail of his eye, as he drew level, he saw a legionary of the gate guard begin to raise his arm. With his mouth suddenly dry, as though he had bitten a sloe, he reached out familiarly, and laid a hand which he prayed might not be resented on the bony rump of the little donkey. It was not resented, and the legionary, who had merely developed a sudden itch, was rubbing his nose as though he meant to rub it off.

He was through ! A few paces more, the torchlight falling away behind him, and drawing aside from the old man and the donkey, he strode forward into the night, following the road to Rimini, past the white tombs and black-feather cypress trees and huddled hovels that surrounded Rome, while the traffic thinned as carts and donkeys and mule-trains turned off down side-tracks that led to farms and market-gardens.

Just beyond the third milestone, the road to Rimini dipped steeply to a bridge across the Tiber, and then swung right, following the willow-fringed banks, while the Clodian Way, branching from it, held straight on, climbing steeply to the north. Crossing the tawny river, Beric held straight on also, following the Clodian Way up on to higher ground, and then, with sunrise not far away, got off the road and took to the hills.

He was making for the great coast road, the Aurelian Way. He could have gone out of Rome by that road, and followed it at a safe distance, from the outset: he knew the first few miles well enough, for he had been out that way several times when exercising the Piso horses; but it would have meant going right through the fortifications of Janiculum, and making a long loop down to the coast, so that at the end of the day he would be scarcely any farther north than when he set out. Better to push on this way, edging over towards the coast as he went.

Once, when he was out beyond Janiculum with the horses, he had seen a cohort of the Legions come swinging down the road, marching with a steady, formidable stride that looked as though it had not changed its rhythm in a thousand miles. Watching the Cohort Commander swing by, the lean, brown, dusty men behind him, he had wondered idly to a farmer who had drawn aside like himself, to give them right of way, where they had come from. 'By the charging boar on their standard,' the man said; ' they'll be a Cohort of the Twentieth —stationed in Britain, so I've heard, and has been for nigh on a hundred years.'

And Beric had gazed after them until the dust rose between him and the baggage-train; and then turned to look away up the long paved road by which they had come, with the

sudden homing hunger twisting in his stomach : and asked,
' Then could you get to Britain, just by following that road? '

'I could if I was fool enough,' the farmer had said, and
spat into the ditch.

Beric had no real hope that, alone and hunted and without
money, he would get back to Britain by following the Aurelian
Way or any other; but he turned homeward blindly, without
thought, obeying the same instinct that draws the wild geese
northward in the spring.

The sun slid up over the landward rim of the hills, with a
suddenness that still seemed strange to Beric, used to the long
twilights of the north. One moment the world was dark, and
the next the darkness had become a bloom of shadow like the
bloom on a grape, and the sky overarching it was filling with
light that strengthened and strengthened until it seemed to
sing. And then the light spilled over, splashing through the
still bare oakwoods and trickling in runnels of rose and gold
down the glens of the distant Apennines. Colour sprang out
in the world, the silvery, dusty colours of the south; the soft
grey-green of olive trees, the thunderous darkness of the pines.
Birds were singing among the climbing oak-woods, and here
and there the dark carpet of ivy under the trees was flecked
with tiny pink cyclamen. And as he climbed, Beric could feel
the sun warm on his back.

Behind him, in Rome, the hunt would be up now.

Gradually, as though the sun's warmth was thawing something in him back to life, he began to wake up. Ever since
the moment last night when he had come to himself in the dark
store-room, with the horror of the salt-mines upon him, he
seemed to have been acting in obedience to some part of himself that did not usually do his thinking for him. Now he was
thinking for himself again, and looking back over the night,
nothing of it seemed quite real save for the few moments that
he had stood outside Valarius's house, to bid good-bye to the
Lady Lucilla. It was now, also, that he realized his empty
stomach. But there was nothing to be done about that at
present, so he did his best to forget it.

Hour after hour he held on, working steadily over towards the coast, through a land of marshy valleys and steep wooded ridges, from the crests of which, as the day wore on, he began to catch occasional glimpses of the sea.

Towards evening, climbing yet another ridge, he checked among the pine trees on the crest, looking down on a little farm lost among the hills; a stream running by it, fringed with willows that were blurred with the powdery gold of leaf-buds. Odd that he had not noticed, back there in Rome, that the spring was coming. Surely the Piso garden should have told him; but narcissi and anemones were alien flowers having no message for him, whereas a budding willow was a thing he knew and understood. Last year he had known, even in Rome, when the spring was coming in, but unhappy though he had been last year, he had not been Glaucus's slave.

More than once, that day, he had come to the edge of cultivation, and always he had turned aside, keeping to the woods; but he was so weary, and in such desperate need of food; his light sandals were long since worn through and it was so long since he had gone barefooted that his feet were cut and bleeding; and this little lost farm in the wilderness could surely hold no danger for him. It looked a poor farm, a mere huddle of rudely thatched sheds, a few olives and ill-kept vines on the terraced hillside, a ragged pumpkin patch, a small herd of goats grazing unattended; a small, stubborn clearing among the encroaching tide of juniper and lentisk, wild vine and broom and rosemary, that seemed to clothe all the open spaces among these hills, and swept right to the back wall of the steading. But a feather of smoke rose from the house-place into the evening air, and as Beric hesitated on the ridge, his ears full of the æolian hum of pines, a woman came out from behind one of the out-buildings, carrying a bucket—a woman in a tunic that was the faded blue of day-old flax flowers.

There was something so homely in the sight that Beric's mind seemed to make itself up for him, and almost before he knew it he was out from under the pines, and stumbling wearily downhill towards her.

X

THE FARM IN THE HILLS

THE woman glanced up and saw him coming, then
looked quickly and uncertainly towards the house, and
up at him again, in a way that suggested, even at that
distance, that she was startled—as well she might be, Beric
thought, for it was not likely that many strangers found their
way up here among the hills. Then she set the bucket down,
and stood waiting for him, hands on hips.

'Good fortune on the house, and on the woman of the
house,' Beric greeted her courteously when, having found his
way between the goat-fold and the fly-loud dung-heap, he
reached the farm-yard.

'Good fortune they need, with the master of the house
forever off on his own affairs and leaving the vines to go to
ruin,' said the woman. She was a little wizened rat of a
woman, with a narrow, fierce face, but her manner, though
harsh, was not unfriendly as she looked at Beric. 'If you have
business with my man, you have come on a fool's errand, for
he is from home, as usual.'

Beric shook his head. 'I have no business with your man.
I am going north to—to see my sister who is sick; and I must
have missed my way, and seeing this place——'

'If it is the Aurelian Way you've missed, you have indeed.
It is three miles and more over yonder,' the woman inter-
rupted, pointing. 'You will hardly get back to it before dusk,
and there is no inn before the next Twenty-mile station.'

Beric's mouth twisted a little. 'The lack of an inn is small
odds to me, for I have no money. I—I came away in something of a hurry, you see.'

The woman looked at him shrewdly, uncomfortably
shrewdly, but with a sort of contemptuous kindliness. 'So

you came away in something of a hurry, did you? And by the looks of you, somebody tried their best to stop you coming away at all.' Then, as Beric remained silent, she laughed. ' Nay now, I've no interest in what you are nor how you came away. What is it that you want? '

Beric's gaze dropped to the bucket. There was milk in it, as he had hoped there might be. ' If you could spare me a drink of milk,' he said, ' and some rags to tie up my feet. It is a long time since I went barefoot.'

The woman glanced down, noticing the tattered remains of the light sandals he wore, and the spot of blood oozing out from a cut under his big toe; and her fierce face softened a little. ' You can have your drink of milk,' she said, almost defiantly, 'and the rags. I have work waiting for me in the house, and if you will fold the goats and do one or two other odd jobs for me so that I can get on with it, I will give you a bite to eat, too; and you can sleep the night in one of the out-houses.' And she gave him the bucket and let him drink his fill of the warm, sweet goat's milk. Then, telling him, ' You will have no trouble with the goats if you whistle for them. See to them first, and come and tell me when it is done,' she took back the bucket, and with a final fierce nod departed into the house.

Almost dizzy with relief and weariness combined, Beric set himself to fold the goats, which was done easily enough, for at his first whistle the big herd billy came down to the fold of his own accord, with his she-goats and their kids behind him. At the woman's order he fetched water from the stream, and broke up and brought in wood for the house from the wood-pile; and then she called him in to his promised supper.

The smoke-blackened house-place had the same depressed and ramshackle air as the whole farm, but a cheerful fire burned in the hearth from which some of the smoke found its way out through a hole in the roof, while the rest hung in a dense blue cloud among the rafters. And the woman pointed Beric to a stool beside the fire, and gave him barley bread and strong goat's milk cheese and radishes so hot that they brought tears to his eyes. She let him eat in peace, and asked no question, and he was unutterably grateful.

The food put fresh life into him, and presently he began to look about him, and notice things that he had been too dazed with weariness to notice at first; small things, that puzzled him. He noticed that the little fierce woman, who had sat down to her spinning, had her faded and dirty tunic clasped at the shoulder with a brooch of goldsmith's work that he did not think the Lady Poppaea would have been ashamed to wear. He noticed that a shawl over a nearby chest against the wall—though it too was dirty—was a thing of flower-petal colours, glimmering with silver thread. It seemed strange that such things could have come from the profits of a half-derelict farm. The wine that she had given him in an earthen cup was not the sour, muddy stuff that he would have expected, either. And surely there were more benches and stools about than seemed likely—as though there was often company here. . . .

And then the warmth and food combined into a sleepiness that welled up in him, so that he noticed nothing more.

He found that it was dark, and the woman had lit a little lamp and was telling him impatiently to come with her, and he got up like an obedient dog, and lurched after her. She opened a door at the far end of the room, and led him through, holding the lamp high. 'You can sleep here,' she said. 'I'll dare swear you have slept in worse places.'

Looking hazily round him in the lamplight, Beric thought that he certainly had. It was a storeroom of sorts, but not disused like the one in which he had been imprisoned last night. Flour-baskets were stacked in one corner, the earthen floor moon-pale around their bases; there were oil-jars, and a few spare farm implements, a stack of yellow dried pumpkins, a couple of tall wine-jars in a rough stand. In another corner were a pile of rough-dressed goat-skins with the hair still on them, and the woman pointed to these. 'You can make yourself a bed there: don't go damaging the skins. I want to sell them. You shall have some rags for your feet in the morning.'

And before Beric could get out a sleep-blurred word of thanks, she was gone. The door rattled to behind her, and he was alone in the dark. Taking his direction from the pale window-square high in the wall, he groped his way over to the corner she had pointed out, and lay down, rolling himself in his cloak and pulling a couple of the ill-smelling skins over him. The door was a bad fit, and from where he lay he could see a broad crack of gold all down one side of it, which was a friendly thing to see in the darkness. He stretched out, settling his head on his arm, and the warm black waves of sleep engulfed him.

How long he slept, he had no idea. He woke with a crash, to a confusion of sounds: to loud voices and tramping footsteps beyond the ramshackle door, and a sense of danger thrusting in out of the night. One of the voices was that of the woman, raised and startled.

'Milo! I thought you were working the Alban Hills! What in the name of Typhon brings you back into these parts so soon?'

A man's voice answered, with a deep, reckless note of laughter in it. 'What but your bright eyes, Rhodope?'

The woman gave an impatient snort. 'I suppose you have run into trouble.'

'Trouble enough,' another voice answered, grumblingly. 'We got word of a rich caravan, but Florus mishandled his end of the business, and when we came on them they had twice the escort we were prepared for. So we lost Carpus and the Cyclops, and got not so much as a denarius or a dab of spikenard in exchange. And now Junius has split the band up again, until the breeze dies out.'

'So here we come, back to our old hunting grounds,' a third voice cut in. 'And behold'—there was a brutal laugh, and a jingling as of a bag of coins being rattled up and down— 'the luck changes on the first day. The small bands are best, after all.'

'Put it in the usual place,' said the woman. 'And don't tempt your luck by crowing about it.'

'You seem not overjoyed to see us, Rhodope.' It was the man she had called Milo. 'Would you by any chance have been entertaining a Tribune of the Watch, behind our backs?'

Rhodope laughed, half angrily. 'You startled me. I was not expecting you, and I thought you might be robbers.'

There was a roar of appreciation at the jest, and Beric, lying rigid on his elbow in the dark, realized that there must be six of the men at the very least.

'Well, now that you *are* here, I suppose you will be wanting food,' the woman said ungraciously.

'Food! Yes—food and wine: much wine!' several voices answered her, rising together in a ragged clamour that had unmistakably the note of the wolf-pack in it. 'Bring us wine, Rhodope—much wine to keep us happy while you make ready the food!' There was a confused sound of stools and benches being scraped on the earthen floor, and men flinging themselves down and stretching out their legs, and the chink and rattle of weapons being laid aside.

When Rhodope spoke again, it was from just outside the store-room. 'You can start on what is in that jug. I'll be back with some more before it is empty.' She opened the door and slipped quickly through, closing it behind her, and next instant she was bending over Beric, who, doing the only thing he could think of, had dropped flat and shut his eyes as she opened the door. He could hear her breathing, and the light of the lamp she carried shone red through his closed lids. There was a moment's tingling pause, and then, 'No need to pretend to be asleep,' she whispered. 'None but the dead could sleep through this uproar.'

Beric opened his eyes, screwing them up against the swimming dazzle of light, and saw her face hovering over him, fierce as a dagger thrust. 'You are a runaway slave, aren't you?' she whispered. Then savagely, as he made to spring up, 'Lie still, you young fool, if you want to see the sun rise! I'll not give you up to the Watch. I've been a slave myself.

115

Nor I'll not give you up to the wolves in there, because being what you are, you cannot carry tales of this house to the Watch, for the Watch would as lief get their hands on you as they would on us. So you can thank your gods if you have any, for the white mark of the slave ring on your arm, for it has saved your throat to-night. You understand?'

Beric nodded wordlessly.

Someone beyond the door had begun to sing, and the woman glanced toward the sound, and hurried on: 'If they knew you were here, even that would not save you, for they are lads that take no chances: but if you lie still, no harm will come to you, and they will be gone by dawn. Then you can go your way.'

She nodded once, fiercely, as though to drive her point home, and turning away, took down a great jug from a shelf and began to fill it from one of the wine-jars in the corner. The voices in the room were growing impatient, as she reached out to the lamp which she had set down and quenched it. Then she took up the wine-jug and opened the door. The voices seemed to rush in upon Beric, and then fall back again, as it closed behind her.

The men greeted her reappearance with loud complaints that she had been a long time and the jug was empty. 'The glim went out,' Beric heard her say. 'It will have done you no harm to draw breath between swallows.'

'So long as we have the wherewithal to swallow now,' someone said.

For a while Beric lay frozen, every nerve in his body on the stretch, listening to the grumble of voices in the next room, where the men seemed to have settled into a quieter mood than the boisterous one in which they had arrived, catching the smell of frying meat and the strong whiff of garlic, and watching with strained eyes the crack of smoky lamplight down the side of the door. Then his utter weariness overcame him, and uneasily, by fits and starts, he began to drowse. He tried desperately to keep awake, afraid that if he slept he might roll over with a thud or fling out an arm and overset something, and so betray himself. But it was no good: little by little sleep claimed him once more.

Yet again he was roused with a start, this time by the bleating of the big herd billy, taken up by the shriller bleating of the other goats in the fold. Almost in the same instant he heard a startled curse from the next room: a few muttered words followed by swift and stealthy movements, and then the crack of light went out. There was a scraping sound, as of a chest being dragged out from the wall, and a few moments later, dragged back again: and almost before it ceased, there came a quick tramping outside, a crisp order, and then a thunder of blows against the house-place door, that ended in a splintering crash as it burst open, and a rush of heavily shod feet.

Beric was up and crouching by the door by that time, and squinting through the crack. The room was in darkness, save for the red embers of the dying fire, but he could see that it was full of men, and certainly not the men who had been there before.

'Lights!' someone was demanding. 'Licinius, get a *light*, man! Hell and Furies! How can we rout them out in the dark?'

Someone thrust a torch into the red embers, and began to whirl it aloft; and it spluttered into life, casting a fierce and fitful glare on to bronze shoulder-pieces and naked sword-blades, and the crimson crest of a Centurion's helmet. Men were scattering and questing to and fro in obedience to sharply rapped-out orders. 'Typhon take those goats!' the Centurion swore. 'If they had not given the alarm, we should have had the whole pack.'

'We'll have them yet, sir,' said his second. 'They'll not get past the lads outside.'

But Beric had already turned from the door to the high pale square of the window, his one thought to make his escape before it was too late. For the second time in a day and a night he reached for the high sill of a storeroom window, and swung himself up. It was a larger window than the other had

117

been, and he climbed through without trouble, stiff and sore though he was, and dropped literally into the arms of the Legionaries who had drawn a cordon round the house.

'Here's one of 'em, anyhow,' said a cheerful voice, and then sharpening, 'would you now?—Oh, no you don't, my beauty!'

Beric kicked out wildly, and ducked under the man's arm, towards the shelter of the scrub that came near to the steading walls; but another man rose in his path, and as he swerved, the first was upon him from behind, bringing him crashing down. He fought like a mountain cat for his liberty, but more men closed in on him, and despite all his frantic struggling, his arms were twisted behind him, and he was dragged to his feet.

Struggling still, he found himself a little later standing before the Centurion in the torchlit house-place, which now looked as though a hurricane had hit it, and where the chest had been dragged out to reveal a square hole just large enough for a man to crawl through, in the wall behind.

'Here's one of 'em, sir,' his captor repeated.

'One!' said the Centurion disgustedly. 'And the rest clear away, thanks to those cursed goats!' He was a man with a keen, square-chinned face, and he looked the panting captive up and down. 'You young fool,' he said contemptuously. 'It always ends in the galleys or the cross. What did you want to get mixed up with this lot for?'

'I am not——' Beric began furiously, and checked. If he told the truth, and they believed him, he would be handed back to Glaucus, and that would mean the salt mines, more surely than ever now it would mean the salt mines. If he said nothing, he would be condemned as a robber, and that would mean the galleys or the cross. But at least the galleys were better than the salt mines; and the cross? Well, at least that was quick, a few days at most, sometimes only a few hours, if the Centurion in charge were merciful and had his man scourged half dead beforehand. With a sudden calm of complete and utter despair, Beric made his choice. He ceased to

1

struggle against the grip of the Legionaries who held him, shook the hair out of his eyes, and stared back at the Centurion, with his mouth set into a straight, defiant line.

'I suppose you are a runaway slave,' said the Centurion. 'Your kind usually are. Well, it is no affair of ours, unless your master comes forward, and if he does, it won't help you much. How many of you were there? Was Junius the Syrian one of you?'

Beric said no word.

'You'll get nothing out of him, sir,' said his Optio. 'He is dumb-sullen.'

The Centurion shrugged. 'They have their own code, these wolves of the hill. All right, take him away. Tie his hands before him,' and he turned to speak to another man who had just entered.

Beric was thrust back into the storeroom from which he had so lately escaped. His wrists were strapped before him, and he was left in charge of the Legionary who had captured him, while the search for the rest of the band continued. The Legionary was a friendly soul in his way, and seemed to bear Beric no grudge for being a robber, nor for his kick. 'You don't give me no trouble, and I won't give you no trouble, see?' he said, leaning against the door-post and watching his charge by the light of a candle stuck on a shelf.

The words were somehow familiar, and Beric, drooping against the wall and lost in a daze of hopelessness, seemed to hear them across a long distance of time. But they were not quite right, he thought, not quite right. . . . And then he remembered. 'You don't turn difficult, and I don't jerk this rope, see?' Ben Malachi's man had said that, on the evening that Beric was sold into the Piso household. 'You don't turn difficult, and I don't——'

Men came and went through the house-place; outside, they were beating the thick scrub that swept down to the farm walls; but they would not get anyone now. The robbers must have their own ways through the interlacing mass, to the cover of the woods beyond. He was glad that they would not get Rhodope, who had given him food and let him sit by the fire, and hidden him from the others. The goats had stopped bleating. He wondered if the Legionaries had killed them. The sky beyond the little window was beginning to pale to the colour of an aquamarine. Soon it would be day. It would be market day in Rome, he remembered; and he wondered where he would be next market day.

Someone stuck a head in at the door and said, 'Bring him along. We're marching.'

'Any more?' asked Beric's guard, as he straightened up.

The other spat disgustedly. 'Neither hide nor hair of a one. The scrub is riddled with runs.'

They marched Beric out of the storeroom, out of the house. They thrust him into the midst of a score of Legionaries who were falling in in the farm-yard. A defiant bleat sounded from the hillside above, and Beric noticed that the goat-fold was empty. Either the goats had broken out, or someone had contrived to let them out. Maybe that was Rhodope.

The light seemed to be growing very quickly, a fiercer and more fitful light than the dayspring, and snatching a glance over his shoulder as the whole company moved off at the Centurion's order, Beric saw that they had fired the thatch. The flames looked pale, oddly bloodless in the dawn.

.   .   .   .   .

After the semi-darkness of the Mamatine prison in which he had lain for four days, the sunlight was white and blinding. Beric blinked in the brightness of it that seemed to dazzle his whole head instead of only his eyes. He was standing under guard in the courtyard of one of the city's lesser law-courts; he was itching all over with bug-bites, and there was a mistral blowing, blowing stray bits of garbage in from the street to eddy and rustle in corners.

There had been several people tried already that morning, for robbing or fire-raising, giving short weight, or cutting purses in the lower city. It was growing late, and the Magistrate in charge was in a hurry; and now they were trying Beric—trying him as one of the band of Junius the Syrian, which had robbed a merchant on the Aurelian Way six nights ago. The only one, unfortunately, who had been rounded up. The merchant himself, who with his head heavily bandaged had just given evidence, could not swear to it that Beric had been one of the band who had attacked him, but as it had been dusk, and he had been taken by surprise and hit on the head from behind, that proved nothing, and his slaves had been too busy running to be any more help. Not that it mattered very much; the robbery had been carried out by the band of Junius, and Beric was obviously a member of the band—the Centurion who had captured him described how he had been taken trying to escape from the robbers' hide-out. Therefore he must surely be guilty of the robbery. And when the time came for the prisoner's defence, there was none. Beric had wondered sometimes, while he was in prison, what would happen if he could get word to the Lady Lucilla; but anything that the Lady Lucilla might do to help him would deliver him again to Glaucus and the salt-mines, just as surely as though Glaucus himself should chance to walk through the law-court at this moment. Beric had held stubbornly to his choice, all these five days, but now suddenly he wished that he had not, and a wild fear of what was coming rose in him. If it should be the cross! From the salt-mines he might escape—no one ever did, but still, he might—but if it were the cross there would be no time.

He started forward, opening his mouth to cry out that he was not a robber, that he was a slave of the house of Publius Lucianus Piso, and had run away, and that he was in the farm when it was raided only because the woman Rhodope had given him shelter for the night. But one of his guards drove a hand across his mouth, bidding him shut it, and the moment passed.

And now the judge, who was certainly in a hurry, was summing up. He was a very large man with a puffy face that looked as though it was made of tallow, and a fretful manner;

he was behind time, and Jupiter alone knew when he would get home to his midday meal, for even when the wretched youth had been found guilty, there would still be the matter of his sentence to settle.

He thought about the sentence while he waited in mounting impatience for the jury to make up their minds. He would have liked to make it the cross, as some relief for his feelings at being kept from his waiting meal; but he was a conscientious man. The boy was obviously strong and built for endurance, and since the plague in the autumn the Navy was temporarily a little short of galley-slaves.

The jury had made up their minds and were casting their votes by marked tablets dropped into a jar. An official brought the jar and set it before the Judge, and began to count.

' Guilty ! '

Beric licked dry lips and waited, while the Judge and his assistants bent their heads together. Then the moment came; and the Judge turned his tallowy face full upon him. ' Prisoner, for the hideous crime of which you have been convicted, we sentence you to the galleys, there to row at the oar, henceforth until your life's end.'

Beric had wondered what he would feel when the moment came. He felt nothing. He noticed very clearly the exact colour—grey-blue over milky green—of a wilting cabbage leaf which the mistral had blown against the foot of a column nearby, the sharply frilled edge of it, and the rim of shadow that followed its outline so faithfully underneath. He knew that he would never forget the colour of that cabbage leaf, nor the way the big veins branched, nor the rim of shadow under the edge.

XI

THE *ALCESTIS* OF THE RHENUS FLEET

THE wide waters of the Rhenus caught the first shrill
gleam of the early northern sunlight, flashing silver as
it flowed out from the mist-haunted darkness of the
forest, and lapped along the river ramparts and the jetties
of Colonia Agripensis. On the west bank—the Roman bank
of the river—the little colonial town, capital of the Lower
Rhenus Province, sat compactly within its walls, with the
usual native fringe huddled about it, and the big camp that
was the winter station of the Twenty-second Legion; its
cleared cornland, and the vineyards where the vines were in
young leaf. On the far bank stretched the forests and the
marshes of Barbarian Germany, and between them flowed the
broad river, the frontier along which passed and re-passed the
patrol galleys of the Rhenus Fleet.

This morning a small convoy of transports lay at anchor in
midstream, their stocky shapes in marked contrast to the long,
lean lines of the two naval galleys who were their escort; and
the ordered bustle aboard both transports and galleys alike
made it clear that they were sailing almost at once.

A group of men came out through the turreted river-gate
of the town, three of them in the bronze and crimson of the
Legions, the rest clearly officials, and strolled down the jetty,
talking together.

' A very fine lot, this year,' said a little plump man whose
many-folded toga showed the purple stripe of a Magistrate.
' Yes, I flatter myself, an unusually fine lot, especially our big
tall lads of the Lower Province.'

' Oh, of course, if size were the *only* thing that counted for
the Eagles.' The man in the gilded bronze of a Legate,
pacing beside him, gave a sharp, snapping laugh. ' No; far

be it from me to set my stranger's ignorance against your so-
many years experience of these provinces. I admit that on the
parade-ground yesterday I was more impressed by the Upper
Province drafts; but in that I may well have been influenced
by the commonly held opinion that hillmen make the best
soldiers, all the world over.' He noticed, and did not care,
that the Provincial Governor's plump face looked like that of a
baby who has been slapped without cause. He had spent all
yesterday evening with the Governor, listening to his ceaseless
self-congratulations on the infinite superiority of the Lower
Province and everything in it; and had reached the stage
where the man's simplest remark annoyed him.

Behind them, he could hear the town waking to the new
day. The sun was rising higher, drawing out the resiny
sweetness of the pinewoods, and the light wind smelled warm
and tangy, a forest wind. Cornelius Chlorus, the new Legate
of the Second Augustan Legion, sniffed it, but without
pleasure. He was tired of German forests; swampy, mist-
shrouded, rain-drenched German forests. His mind went
back over the long tour of inspection that had brought him
all up the Limes and the Rhenus defences, in what seemed,
looking back on it, to have been ceaseless rain. Three half-
drowned months. Well, Jupiter be praised, they were over.
Now he had only to pick up the new Rhenish drafts, and pro-
ceed with them to Britain, to take over his command. He had
inspected the new drafts, and seen them marched aboard
last evening; tall, raw-boned, barley-haired lads, mostly
descended from the Legions—the Second among them—who
had served here under Agrippa and Germanicus, and married
wives and settled when their service was over. Now it was
time that he went aboard himself.

As he reached the edge of the jetty, with his two young staff
officers behind him, the trumpet sounded from one of the
galleys, clear and sweet across the water. She had weighed
anchor a short while before, and lay with her oars moving just
sufficiently to keep her station against the current. Now her
bow came round, the beat of her oars growing suddenly quick

and purposeful as her rowers sent her speeding in towards the jetty. She was a low-set forty-oar galley, carrying her oars in a single tier—the towering triremes of the south would be useless in the steep northern seas—and for the first time, as he watched the lean, swift lines of her and the perfect precision with which her oars rose and fell, a gleam of pleasure showed in the hard face under the eagle-crested helmet of the Legate.

On she came at racing speed, the water curling back from her bow above the deadly underwater ram, the seamen and marines standing ready at their stations, the tall figure of the Master alone on her foredeck; on until it looked as though she must ram the jetty. Then, at seemingly the last instant, the Master's hand flashed up. The gesture was echoed by the Hortator—the rowing master—seated at the break of the poop, and in perfect unison the oar-blades dropped, and held water.

'Percol! You would expect her to rear like a horse!' said one of the staff officers, in quick admiration, as the galley came to a shuddering halt amid a turmoil of white water.

'Surely. The Master knows his job,' nodded the Legate.

The Master's hand fell, and again the Hortator echoed the movement, this time with a sweeping gesture. Again the rowers bent to their oars; but now those on the steerboard side backed while those on the larboard gave way; and the galley came about in her own length. For the first time the Master's voice sounded. 'Way enough.' The oars slid fore and aft, and she settled lightly, broadside on, to the fenders.

Seamen sprang to secure her, and to run out the boarding-bridge, and the trumpeter stood ready to sound as the Legate stepped on board, while on the jetty the Legate himself, belatedly remembering his manners, had turned to take a courteous leave of the Provincial Governor and his officials. And on the crowded rowing-benches, the galley slaves dropped over their oars, motionless, as though they had no life save in rowing and when they ceased to row the life went out.

Sixth from the bow on the steerboard side, Beric sat slumped in his place like the rest.

It was almost two years since he came north with many others sentenced to the galleys, to fill the gaps in the Rhenus Fleet. He knew that, because it had been late spring when first he was shackled to the rowing-bench, and there had been another spring since then, and now it was spring again. The scent of the sun-warm pine-woods blowing down the little wind was not quite lost, even in the reek which rose from the close-packed rowing benches of the *Alcestis*. Once—even last spring—it had stirred old longings in Beric and hurt him unbearably, but then he had been only a year with the galleys: now he had been two, and he was beyond the hurt of such things.

He scarcely ever thought of Lucilla now, nor of old Hippias, nor even of Gelert, his dog. He thought of Glaucus sometimes, because it was pleasant to hate; and he thought what a fool he had been to refuse Glaucus his help over the mare. What had possessed him to be such a fool? He could not remember, and he did not try. What did such things as thine and mine matter, after all? If you were stronger than your neighbour, you grabbed: it was as simple as that. He was not above stealing somebody's share of the black beans and rotten dried figs and sour wine when the food came round—so long as Jason, his oar-mate, did not go short thereby. They all grabbed more than their share when they got the chance, for they were always hungry. At feeding time they would howl like dogs, Beric as loudly as any, baying for the black beans and sour wine passed round from bench to bench. Sometimes the rowers of three or four benches—more could not reach each other, because of their ankle-chains—would fight like dogs over the food, until parted like dogs by the argos-eyed overseer who strode whip in hand up and down the flying-deck between the benches.

Beric lifted his head a little, and looked aft towards the poop before which the Hortator sat at his sounding-table. He saw pair beyond pair of bowed backs, naked and gaunt, striped with scars of the whip-lash. Lybian and Scythian, golden Greek and black Ethiopian, Jew and Goth and Gaul;

127

the sweepings of the Empire, shackled like himself, each by an ankle to his bench and a wrist to his oar-mate. Some of them had been here when Beric was first chained among them; some were new-comers; there were always fresh slaves coming in to fill the places of those that wore out and died. You could often tell how long a slave had been at the oar by the look of him, not merely by the age and number of the scars on his back, nor by his gauntness, his cracked and blackened skin, and the depth of his shackle-galls, but by the gradual going out of everything behind his eyes, like the slow going out of a light. After a time, everything went out. Maybe it was better that way, better when one stopped thinking. It did not happen always; it had not happened to Beric, so far, and for good or ill, in some way that he did not understand, he knew that that was because of Jason.

On the jetty, the Legate was still taking an elaborate leave of the officials, while the galley waited with her boarding bridge run out and her seamen and marines drawn up in array. Well, so long as the waiting lasted, one did not have to row. The Legate could take all day and a hundred days over his farewells, for all Beric cared. Once he did come aboard there would be little enough rest for the rowers, until they brought him and his clean and beardless Tribunes to their journey's end. For the first time Beric wondered where it was they were bound for, with the troop transports; but the question had no interest for him, and he let it fall.

Beside him, Jason gave a little strangled cough, and then was silent again. The overseer glanced towards him with a suggestive flick of the long lash he held. But Jason did not again mar the silence of the well-disciplined galley. Beric, with a sudden twinge of fear, moved his hand outward a little on the smooth oar-loom, and as though in reassurance, the gaunt hand of his oar-mate shifted to meet it. For an instant hand touched against hand in comradeship, and shifted apart again.

Jason had been there when Beric came. He was a Greek, and a painter. 'When you have set the last touch to the last

128

bright feather of your flying bird, and you step back to look, and say to your own heart " I have made a thing, and it is beautiful ", that is a fine time,' he had told Beric, on the only occasion on which he had ever spoken of himself: ' The finest time in life, except perhaps the moment when you come to your untouched wall, and the flying bird is still in your heart.' He had come to Rome to make his fortune, but he had not made it, because Rome did not want the sort of frescoes he painted. ' I could never paint a fat goddess on a cloud; I had sooner catch the whistling swiftness of wild geese over-head.' He had lived wildly, and backed Leek Green at the Chariot Races when Scarlet had had all the luck. Finally he had been taken in payment for a debit, and sold into slavery. And when it had dawned on him that he was a slave, he had gone berserk, and attacked the man who had made him one. The man had been a Senator, and Jason had gone to the galleys.

For two years he and Beric had pulled at the same oar, up and down the Rhenus and along the North Sea shores. They had laboured and eaten and slept together, like a yoke of oxen which, once joined, labour and graze and lie down linked together by their yoke-chains, until one of them dies. It was very seldom that they could speak to each other. That brief, wordless contact of hand against hand on the oar-loom had to do instead; and it had come to do well enough.

All that seemed left to Beric of decency and faith and kindness was bound up in what he felt for the Greek beside him, and every time Jason gave that little exhausted cough, Beric suffered the same stab of fear.

But now at last the Legate was coming aboard, followed by his staff. The Master and the Centurion of Marines stepped stiffly forward to greet him at the head of the boarding bridge, the clashing Roman salute was exchanged, and the trumpet sang as he set foot on deck. From his place on the reeking rowing-benches Beric watched the little scene on the poop, the ordered movements, the fierce glint of gilded bronze and crimson horsehair in the morning sunlight, as though it

were something happening in another world. The tall man
with the eagle-crested helmet had turned to glance along the
rowing-benches. 'You have your rowers well trained,'
Beric heard him say to the Master. 'I never saw the
manœuvre better carried out.'

He should have said that to Porcus, Beric thought, with
a savage twist of the mouth. To Porcus, the overseer, whose
whiplash had given them their training: might his soul rot
for it! He heard the crisp ring of orders, and the seamen ran
to their new stations; the Hortator raised his hammer, and
all along the benches the rowers tensed to their oars. 'Let
go' and 'Shove off' came the orders, and the galley gave a
little resilient shudder and swung out from the fenders as they
were obeyed. 'Clack!' came the hammer on the sounding-
table, and the forty long oars dipped as one.

The Legate on the poop turned and flung up an arm in final
farewell to the knot of officials on the jetty, and the Governor,
answering the gesture, called across the widening water:
'Fair winds to Britain, Cornelius Chlorus!'

The words, meant for the Legate, came also to the straining
rowers. Beric heard them with a sense of shock, as though the
oar had bucked under his ribs. Fair winds to Britain! Fair
winds home! Suddenly the longing for his own hills, which
had dulled in him like so much beside, woke to a wild and
frenzied beating, and the bitterness of despair rose in his
throat and choked him. He came out of the blind moment
to see his own hands and Jason's on the swinging oar-loom, and
the blue glint of the light on their irons.

The *Alcestis* was in her place now at the head of the little
convoy, while her sister the *Janiculum* lay watchful at the tail;
and all down the line the transports were weighing anchor,
the brilliant sails unfurling to the light following breeze.
Beric would have known when the *Alcestis*' sail was set, even
if he could not see the wind-filled curve of it bending to the
low mast, orange-scarlet against the pine-woods and the
milky sky; he would have known it by the sudden sense of
increased purpose and buoyancy. He knew every mood and

condition of the *Alcestis* by this time, as though she were a mare. Every sound of her, every sight and smell, every variation of her behaviour in different seas had entered into him and become part of himself; just as the feel of the oar that he and Jason had pulled for two years, the great firwood oar kept white with pumice stone and the wash of the seas, had become part of himself.

On the fore-deck the fleet altar had been set up, and before it the Legate had made offerings to Neptune for a prosperous voyage, and the sharp sweetness of incense drifted down to the rowers from the altar behind them.

Now the voyage was begun in earnest; the marines and seamen who were not on duty had gone below, and the Legate and his staff had disappeared into the cabin under the poop. On the flying-deck between the banks of rowers, the overseer had begun his ceaseless prowling to and fro, his narrow eyes alert for any excuse to use the long lash he handled with such skill. Every now and then he would find the excuse he sought, and the lash would flicker out like dark lightning, and some poor wretch would yelp with pain as it seared across his straining shoulders. The beat of the Hortator's hammer setting the rowing pace when needful, the leathery creak of the oars working against their oaken thole-pins, the dip of the blades, and the slap and ripple of water along the galley's sides; there were the sounds of the *Alcestis* under way. These, and the never-ceasing sob, rising and falling with the rhythm of the oars, ' Huyha! Huyha! ' that rose from the lungs of her rowers.

All the long daylight hours it went on, the whiplash and the water-sounds and the sobbing breaths of the rowers, until night came, and the convoy anchored, until morning again made it possible to navigate the river-shoals. Four days the convoy worked slowly downstream, down from forest country into marsh; at last into the maze of waterways of the Rhenus delta, with its sudden mists, its shifting shoals and mud banks among which they must nose their way to the sound of the leadsman's call, its swift and treacherous currents among low, marshy islands. And on the fifth evening they anchored off the last station of the Rhenus Fleet, a mere huddle of low timber buildings and a repair yard, sheltered by turf banks from the fury of wind and sea alike. And there the water-casks and wine-jars were replenished, and fresh meat brought on board.

On that last night there was meat even for the rowers, beside their usual black beans and sour wine. The Overseer and his Second brought it round in great baskets, and flung it to them, ragged lumps of it. It was half raw, it showed red and black in the lantern light, and it stank; but they bayed for it like dogs.

Beric got a larger lump than most, but found to his disgust that more than half of it was bone. It was useless to protest. He tore off what flesh there was with his teeth, and swallowed it more or less whole, then looked round for any other fragment that might be torn from its rightful owner. As he did so, Jason produced his own share, scarcely touched, shielding it from the sight of the rest. 'Take it,' he said.

Beric's hand went out involuntarily, then dropped back. 'No, it is yours,' he muttered.

'I do not want it. I have dined over-well on black beans already.' Jason's voice still held a glint of the reckless laughter it must once have possessed.

'Eat it quickly, or you will not have the chance.'

The other shook his head. 'Truly I have no stomach for it. I cannot eat. I——' His words ended in the little exhausted cough that his oar-mate had come to dread.

Instantly Beric was kneeling over him. 'Eat!' he demanded roughly, the old fear leaping in his voice. 'You must eat; it will give you strength.' He took the lump of meat and hurriedly began to tear it into pieces. 'Now—it will go down easier now.' He thrust the first piece back on Jason, who took it without more protest, and made shift to swallow it, though with an effort.

But by that time their neighbours were awake to what was happening. 'Nay, if his belly is too full, there be others still empty,' said the guttural voice of the Hun who rowed at the next oar, and his eager hand came out to snatch.

Beric struck it away with a curse, and thrust more of the meat on Jason. 'Eat again,' he said urgently; and then, as another hand came out, flung its owner back with his shackled arm. 'Oh, son of Set! Keep your filthy claws to yourself!' And next instant a small snarling dog-fight was in being, as the rowers from the bench on either side flung themselves on Beric and Jason.

There came a rush of feet along the flying-deck, and the vicious crack of a whip. 'Dogs! Vermin!' Porcus shouted above the sudden uproar. 'Spawn of Typhon! Off! Off, I say! Get back!' Again and again the lash curled into their midst. Beric felt it sear like a hot iron across his shoulder as the fight fell sullenly apart, and he stumbled up to his knees.

He found himself staring up into the disdainful face of the Legate, who had evidently been drawn from his cabin by the noise. For a moment their eyes met, and then the Legate turned, and in his cool, impatient voice cut into the Overseer's raging as he spoke to the Hortator who was also upon the scene. 'Your cattle are unruly; you should not have given them meat, my friend.'

It was the Master's voice that answered. 'That was done by my orders, sir. Before a long trip such as lies ahead of us, meat is good for the rowers; it puts stomach into them.'

'Too much stomach, and that too high,' snapped the Legate. 'Meat-fed rowers are a menace; I have had trouble with such before now. Let there be no more meat fed to these while I am aboard.'

'There will, of course, be no more until the eve of the return voyage, sir,' said the Master a little stiffly; then to the Hortator, 'All's over. You can get below again, Rufus.' Lastly he spoke to the rowers. 'Lie down, you fools. If there is another sound out of you to-night, I'll have the hide flayed off every tenth man in the morning.'

Then he was gone, and the Legate also. The Hortator and the Overseer had betaken themselves to their own places:

only the Officer of the Watch stood alone on the foredeck, his cloaked figure dark against the sky.

Muttering and growling, the galley-slaves stretched out under the benches, and quiet settled down. Beric and Jason lay huddled close together for warmth. Voices came up from the quarters of the crew and the marines below, and a laugh spilled out with the yellow lantern-light from the Legate's cabin. The sound of singing stole across the water from one of the transports and was taken up by the rest; the drafts on board were clearly overwhelmed by the knowledge that this was their last night in their own river. They were singing in their native tongue, but the tune told its own story; exile ached in every note of it. Presently they would be happy again, but to-night they were home-sick, and the voice of their homesickness found a despairing echo in Beric.

A faint mist shimmered low over the water and the marsh; the orange door-squares in the low, dark ranges of the shore buildings went out one by one, and only the stern braziers of the convoy still shone above the mist. The water lapped and whispered along the dark sides of the galley, and the rowers moaned and muttered in their sleep. And still Beric lay wakeful. A few days ago the singing across the water would have had no power to hurt him, but that had been before he knew that they were bound for Britain. And it hurt now.

Jason stirred beside him with a long, heavy sigh. Jason had eaten some of the meat before the fight started. That was good. One thing that was good, anyway. And oddly comforted by the thought, Beric turned over, his chain jinking as he did so, and laid his arm across Jason, and almost at once was asleep.

XII

STORM AT SEA

THE tide was on the turn, and aboard the *Alcestis* and her sister galley the rowers had been fed again, and were already at their oars. But on the poop the Legate stood with the Master and the pilot in hasty conference.

Beric, watching the little intent group before the high stern, knew well enough what it was that held them there in low-voiced conclave. He knew the weather signs: the signs of clouds and flying birds, of sounding surge and the indefinable smell of coming tempest in the wind. Were they to sail on this tide? That was the question being decided up there on the poop. The Master shook his head once doubtfully, but it seemed the Legate was in a hurry; he would always be in a hurry, that one, Beric thought, watching the handsome, impatient face under the crested helmet. There could never be any patience in him. He would make a bad hunter.

Now the Council had reached its decision, and clearly it was the one the Legate wanted. The ship's officers saluted and went quickly to their own stations. The *Alcestis*'s trumpet sounded and was echoed back across the water from the *Janiculum*, then from the transports. Instantly the whole convoy sprang from its waiting stillness into activity; seamen ran to their stations, orders were hailed from ship to ship. On board the *Alcestis*, Porcus was already on the prowl as the oars were run out and secured by their leather thongs to the thole-pins. The anchor was weighed dripping over the bow, and the square flame-red sail with its black eagle fell from the standing yard, curving out to the light wind as it was sheeted home. And again Beric felt that instant response of the galley, as the steersman put over the double rudder, and she slipped forward, heeling a little as wind and tide took her.

One behind another, the transports slipped from their anchorage, their striped sails set; lastly the *Janiculum* swung into line. On the rough landing-stage and along the shore of the repair yard, small figures, growing smaller every moment, turned from their work to watch the convoy slip out on the morning tide, nosing through the last shoal-waters to the open sea.

Five hours before noon, with the coast growing cloud-faint behind the tail of the convoy, half the rowers were stood off. That was always the way during long passage rowing which must go on day and night. There was no space to carry two teams of rowers, let alone the difficulty of chaining and unchaining such unruly cattle, and the danger that they would be to the galley when free of their benches. So until they dropped anchor in Dubris Harbour under the green British downs it would be like this, one man to each oar rowing, while the other slipped beneath the bench and got what sleep he could, turn and turn about in four-hour watches.

Beric had that first watch, while Jason lay huddled at his feet. It passed uneventfully: a long monotony of effort; the dip and the long heave back with one's feet braced, the rise and fall again of the white-fir oar-blades that caught the sunlight in an instant's dazzle with every stroke; the long swing of the grey North Sea swell.

An hour before noon the inner watch was relieved, and it was Jason's turn to row, while Beric lay down on the deck, exchanging the grey seas for the windy sky and the flaming curve of the sail, and Jason's dark figure swinging to and fro above him. At mid-afternoon the rowers were changed again, and again at first dark, when they were fed in their separate watches, first those who were just going on to the oars, and then those who had just come off. An hour before midnight Beric stumbled, still half asleep, back to his oar. Towards the end of that watch the wind began to freshen, and the Officer of the Watch spoke a few hurried words to the

Master, who stood beside him, sniffing the weather. But Beric, swinging to and fro in his place, drugged by the unchanging rhythm of effort into a state in which he was barely conscious that he was rowing at all, took no heed of the strengthening easterly breeze; and when, three hours after midnight by the Hortator's hour-glass, the watch was relieved again, he curled up like a dog under the bench and was instantly asleep.

It seemed only a moment later that he woke to the whip-lash searing across his neck, and as he flung up an arm to shield his face, it came again, circling like a white-hot serpent round his wrist. ' Out! Tumble out, you loafing rats!' Naso, the Second Overseer, was shouting. ' Out, and take your share at the oars!' The lash cracked again and again, as Beric, still dazed with sleep and the tumult all about him, stumbled up to his knees; and close beside him someone gave a howl of pain. Naso lurched on down the flying-deck, shouting and laying about him as he went, whipping up the sleepers to join their mates at the bucking oars. As the dazed shock of his awakening cleared from Beric's head and he slipped into his place beside Jason, he realized the uneasy motion of the galley, and the strengthening wind, that had gone round to the north-east. The singing of it was in the rigging, above the creaking and fretting of the galley's timbers, and a burst of salt spray flew in his face; and the oar-loom was alive and kicking under his hands.

Dawn was already breaking, lemon coloured beyond the rents in a hurrying, bat-winged sky, and the grey sea had a tumbling, ruffled look quite unlike yesterday's long swell. Beric was dimly aware of the ordered coming and going of seamen and the Master's voice carrying clear above the wind: ' Man halyards and clewlines,' then, ' Lower away. Clew up!' And men springing to shorten sail, and the flapping of the loosened canvas.

The light strengthened slowly, showing the convoy still well together on a sea that was flecked with white, a sea that ran empty of land to the dipping skyline on every

137

side. As the hours went by the wind strengthened steadily; it hummed in the rigging with a vibrant note like that of a plucked lyre-string; the reefed sail flapped like huge, ungainly wings, and showers of spindrift began to dash over the rowers as they struggled at the oars. Presently the sail was furled as the *Alcestis'* steersman fought to keep her on the course against the wind that was already driving her too far south. For a while, now that the sail was furled, he seemed to succeed, but the wind was still rising, and with more of north in it as the time went by.

But Beric knew only that, with the sea roughening every moment, the oars were becoming unmanageable. 'We must lay the oars in,' he thought over and over again, with growing urgency. 'We *must* lay the oars in!' Porcus, on duty again, came swaying and lurching down the deck, and he shouted to the Overseer, 'We must lay the oars in; some of us will be killed!'

'What matter, so that you row in the meantime?' Porcus shouted back; and *whitt* came the lash across Beric's shoulders so that he plunged at the oar like a horse stung by a hornet. 'Row, you Tiber scum!—Dogs! Offal! Row your hearts out if need be!'

Almost in the same instant, one of the rowers a few benches farther off gave a sharp cry, and slumped groaning over the kicking oar-loom which his mate was struggling to control single-handed.

'There is the first lot of broken ribs for you!' Beric yelled after the Overseer as he lurched off towards the accident.

Porcus and a seaman bent over the groaning wretch. Quite obviously it was true. They would get no more rowing out of this one for a time. While Porcus lurched off to report to the Hortator, who had been at his post since the storm first grew ugly, the seaman half helped, half thrust the injured man from the bench on to the deck, where he stretched out, groaning still. among the feet of the rowers. 'Bring up one of the reserves,' ordered the Hortator. There was no time to unshackle the man now—that must wait until things grew

easier.   He was simply left to lie there, while one of the reserve
rowers, of which every galley carried a few, was brought up
from the hold and thrust into his place.

And the galley drove on, with her complement of rowers
intact once more.

Meanwhile, beside the steersman, on the poop, the Master
and the pilot of the *Alcestis* were confronting the Legate.   'I
dare not hold on like this any longer, sir,' the Master was
saying, respectfully but flatly.   The Legate was the Legate,
and he was only a shipmaster, but on board the *Alcestis* he was
king, and the knowledge stiffened the angle of his grizzled
beard.   'We shall not make Dubris.   We are being driven
farther off our course with every moment that goes by.   The
transports might make it by themselves—they are sailing-
ships, and can tack; we galleys cannot.'

'Galleys are supposed to have rowers,' the Legate pointed
out coldly.

'The rowers are flesh and blood, sir; and flesh and blood
reaches breaking point at last.   Ours have been rowing for
many hours, and the sea is getting up all the time.   Soon we
shall have to begin constant flogging to keep them pulling
their full weight, and presently not even flogging will do it.
And when we reach that point——' He shrugged expres-
sively.   'If we try to keep her to her course any longer, we
shall have the whole convoy on the Barrier Sands in two
hours.'

'That is so, sir,' the pilot put in.   'If we alter course now,
to south-westward, we'll just about shave by, unless the wind
starts to veer.'

For an instant the Legate was silent, his hard face turned
to where, in so few hours now, the shores of Britain should be
lifting over the skyline beyond the galley's prow.   'Very
well,' he said at last, to the two anxious men beside him.
'You are the seamen, and it seems that I have no choice but
to bow to your superior judgement. . . . I shall go below
and try to get some sleep.'   He turned to the poop ladder,
and gathering the beating folds of his cloak about him,

scrambled down it and disappeared with an undignified lurch through the little dark entrance of the cabin.

The two officers glanced at each other in swift relief, and wasted no more time. The Master swung round to a seaman who stood ready for orders. ' Run up the signal for " altering course to larboard " and send someone up to the masthead to make sure that every ship of the convoy receives and answers it.' Then, as the man went to obey, he turned back to the pilot. ' I think we will not make sail.'

The other agreed. ' No, sir: better to use the rowers to get well clear, even if it kills a few of them. Then we can lay the oars in and show a bit of sail and let her run down through the Gaulish Fret. The wind will have gone round to the nor'-west and blown itself out by to-morrow's dawn.'

A long yellow pennant ran up to the masthead, whipping out like a pale bright flame in the wind; and already a man was swinging himself aloft into the tiny fighting-top above the yard. For a short while he remained there, shielding his eyes with his palm. Then he cupped his hands to his mouth, and his hail came down through the tumult of wind and sea and flapping canvas, to the men on the after-deck. ' Signal received by all, sir.'

The Master flung up a hand in reply, then spoke to the steersmen. ' Bring her round.'

' Aye, sir.' The men set their weight to the rudder bar; the great double rudder swung over slowly, and the galley turned in a wide sea-swallow curve through almost the quarter of a circle.

' Steady as you go.'

Beric was instantly aware of the galley's altered course. Her uneasy rolling ceased, she was no longer ploughing diagonally across the seas, but running with them, with a purposeful forward lift up the watery slopes of the waves, and a dip and a slip forward into the troughs like a gull. But that did little to ease the task of the rowers. ' How much longer? ' Beric wondered desperately. ' Do they want to kill us? We *must* lay the oars in! ' And he was not alone in his wondering.

All along the rowing benches there was beginning to be a muttering, that rose soon to a breathless, sobbing outcry. 'We must lay oars in!' someone shouted. 'Fiends out of Tartarus couldn't—row in this—sea!' Someone else took up the cry, and it was echoed and re-echoed back and forth all down the length of the galley. 'Do you want to kill the lot of us? We must lay the oars in—lay the oars—in!'

Porcus was lurching up and down the heaving deck, his whip-lash busy to quell the outcry; but always it broke out again behind him. Then the Master came down from the poop. They saw him speak with the Hortator for a few moments. Porcus rolled up to join them, and stood swaying to the motion of the galley, lithe as a cat, on the balls of his feet. He said something, grinning, with a flash of white teeth in his copper face, and gave a suggestive flick to the lash in his hand. But the Master shook his head impatiently, and turned to look along the banks of rowers.

He flung up his hand to draw their attention, and his voice with the wind behind it carried clear above the tumult, the full length of the galley, so that even the men on the bow benches heard him plainly. 'Listen to me, all of you. It is no use your yelling that the oars must be laid in, that you cannot row. There are fifteen miles of quicksands over yonder.' He pointed over the steerboard bow. 'If we lay the oars in now, the odds are that we shall be on to the southern end of them in something under two hours. Show me that if fiends out of Tartarus couldn't row in this sea, there are eighty galley slaves in the *Alcestis* who can; and when we make Dubris there shall be wine—real wine—and red meat for all of you, as much as you can gorge. If you do not, then the odds are that we shall not make Dubris. That is all.'

Standing there for a moment, after he had finished, his gaze swept challengingly along the rowing-deck. And then a queer thing happened, for sullenly, as though against their wills, the rebellious and exhausted ranks sent up a hoarse and broken shout that might, in free men, have been a cheer.

142

The Master acknowledged it with a flourish of his up-flung arm, and then turned back to the poop ladder.

There was no more outcry on the rowing-benches. The rowers were fighting for their lives; for whatever slim chance there might be for the crew if the galley was wrecked, the slaves, chained to their benches, had none; the life of the galley was quite literally their life too. Yet they were fighting for the galley herself also. They hated the *Alcestis*, and with good cause. She had been a floating hell to them; but they fought for her now as men fight for a thing they love. Half blind with the flying spray, sick and gasping with exhaustion, their hearts bursting in their breasts, they fought the wildly bucking oars, struggling to keep some sort of time to the resonant clack, clack, clack, pulsing through the turmoil of the storm, that was the Hortator's hammer on the sounding-table.

One man was killed at his oar, and three more had ribs broken before at last the order came, ' Stand by to lay in oars.'

A great sob of relief burst from the straining lungs of the rowers as the Hortator's hammer ceased to beat, and they set themselves to the last effort of lifting the oars clear of the thole-pins and laying them in. A few moments later the oars had been housed along the flying-deck, the bulls'-hide storm-shields shipped over the oar-ports, and the *Alcestis* was running before the wind under half sail.

The spent rowers slid numbly from their benches to huddle under the shelter of the bulwarks, their heads down between their heaving shoulders, their backs turned to the wind and the stinging spray of the green following seas. It was not until then that Jason began to cough. It was the same dry, strangled cough that Beric knew of old, but this time it went on and on; and, still coughing, Jason sagged forward on to his face.

Beric caught him in his arms and held him, feeling the small terrible cough rasping through his own body as harshly as through the wasted body of his oar-mate. When it was over, Jason lay quiet against his knees. His eyes were shut, and he was grey-white to the lips as Beric bent over him. 'What is it?' Beric demanded. 'Are you hurt?' His shackled hand was moving hurriedly over the other's chest and sides, feeling for broken ribs. 'Where is the pain? Did the oar catch you?'

Jason opened his eyes. 'No,' he said, quite steadily. 'I am well enough. I felt sick for the moment, and the world—seemed to go far away, that is all. It is coming back now.' He made a weak attempt to sit up, but Beric pressed him back.

'Bide still. Is my knee not a fine enough pillow for you?'

Jason relaxed again, with a ghost of a smile, a twisted, faun's smile that, like his voice, still held the shadow of bygone reckless laughter.

The Hortator and his men were coming round now, un-shackling the dead rower and the injured ones. One of them went over Jason much as Beric had done, but finding no broken ribs, grunted: 'This one is foundered, but he'll be fit to row again when the time comes,' and moved on. Wine was issued to the rowers; real wine, harsh and fiery, and a double ration of black beans. The wine put a little life into them, and warmed them against the chill of exhaustion and the cutting wind-blown spray, and the beans stayed their aching stomachs. Beric poured Jason's share of the wine into him, and a good deal of his own as well, and though it made him choke, it seemed to do him good, so that afterwards he was able to eat some of the black beans which Beric had saved for him in the lap of his drenched and filthy kilt.

The wind was backing steadily but slowly, and the little convoy ran before it, strung out and scattered like a gale-blown skein of geese. On board the *Alcestis* all sense of time had ceased for the rowers, crouching on decks that were awash, with their humped backs to the following seas; there was only a present time of cold and wind and turmoil that seemed to stretch into an eternity. And they did not see, as the day turned towards evening, the dark coastline of Gaul lying low on the tossing skyline, nor know that the gale had gone booming round to the north-west; not even that it was raining.

Beric, still crouching over Jason, so as to shelter him with his own body from the sheets of hissing spray that dashed over the gunwale and forced their way through the shielded oar-ports, slipped gradually into a state between sleeping and waking; an uneasy state in which he seemed to catch ragged glimpses of many dreams, without ever escaping from the tumult all around him; without ever for an instant losing the fear that seemed to twist in his stomach because of Jason.

The light began to fade, and the little convoy, scattered now over miles of sea, was scudding down the coast of Gaul. As the *Alcestis* drew steadily nearer to the shore, the Master and pilot stood together beside the steersman, gazing shoreward as the dark coastline unfurled. 'Keep her out a bit,' the pilot ordered.

And as the steersman eased the rudder over a little, the Master glanced at the man beside him, inquiringly, but without anxiety. He did not know this coast well himself, but he trusted his pilot. The other's face was alert and confident under his leather bonnet; clearly he knew what he was looking for, and was sure of finding it. A green sea broke aft, sluicing all three men with water that could make them no wetter than they were already, and as it foamed across the heaving deck and down among the rowing-benches, the pilot gave a satisfied grunt. 'There she is, sir.'

In the dark wall of the coastline a gap had appeared, which opened wider moment by moment. The pilot gave another order to the steersman, setting his own hand on the kicking rudder bar as he did so, and the galley altered course slightly. The light was going fast, but the gap was widening faster, into the mouth of a great river, and as the *Alcestis* ran towards it, suddenly through the rain-swathes and the deepening twilight a light flared fiercely golden as a marigold, above the darkening headland. 'Ah, there goes the beacon,' the pilot said, hand and eye steady on the business of the moment. 'Best get the sail down and have the oars out again, sir.'

So in the last fading of the gale-torn dusk, the *Alcestis*, with her weary rowers once more at their oars, ran in safely under the flaming beacon at the mouth of the great Gaulish river, and dropped anchor in the comparative shelter of the shore.

XIII

JASON'S ISLAND

ONE by one through the early hours of the night, the rest of the storm-scattered convoy came running in under the beacon on the low headland, until all five lay at anchor in the lee of the wooded shore, sheltered from the full force of the gale that sent the white-capped seas charging in from the river-mouth and drove the hissing rain-swathes before it through the dark. Below decks, the crew and marines grew cheerful over their evening meal, and in the cabin, the Legate had a flask of Falernian broached, but turned in loathing from the cold fried chicken legs provided for him and his staff; and between the rowing-benches the slaves huddled close under the pieces of rotten sail-cloth that had been given them for shelter, too spent to fight over their lumps of greening barley bread.

The gale well-nigh blew itself out in the night, as the pilot had forecast, and dawn broke on a world that seemed utterly spent. The rain had almost stopped, and the stress of the tempest was over, though the woods still moaned and fretted, and the light touched silverly on the heaving swell at the river mouth.

Beric woke to a great crying and calling of shore-birds in the first sodden light, and moved cautiously. The first movement of the day always hurt, for one's shackle-galls and stripes had had time to stiffen while one slept; and this morning it was agony. Every muscle ached, the galls on his wrist and ankle were red raw, while the hardened skin of his hands was rubbed through so that his palms were almost as raw as his shackle-galls, and his breast and belly were a mass of stiffened bruises. Groaning, he dragged himself back to full wakefulness and the weary business of another day. Then he

remembered Jason, and thrusting back the sail-cloth that had
been over his head, came to his elbow with a jerk, and peered
down at his oar-mate.

Jason lay with his head on his arm, his gaunt, bearded face
seeming younger in sleep than it did when he was awake. He
looked very quiet—like a free man, Beric thought, and was
suddenly and piercingly afraid.

But in the same moment, Jason opened his eyes, with a
small bewildered pucker between his brows, as though he had
been in some very different place, and was not yet fully returned to his shackles. Then, as Beric drew a gasping breath
of relief, he rolled over, and lay looking up at him, with the
quietness still in his face.

'What is it?' he asked.

'I was afraid,' Beric said simply.

Jason did not answer at once, but lay studying Beric's face.
Suddenly he smiled, the old twisted faun's smile. 'Oh no,
not that,' he said. 'There are but few things worth being
afraid of, in this world, and assuredly that is not one of them.
Life is none so sweet on the rowing-benches, and death none
so far from any of us who row the great galleys, that we need
pay so much heed to either.'

All around them the huddled wretches were stirring into
life, but for the moment they did not exist for Beric or Jason.
Beric shook the matted hair out of his eyes, and said fiercely:
'Who said it was *that* that I was afraid of? It does not matter
what I was afraid of. You are better, now that you have
slept, and—I will not talk of such things!'

But Jason was not listening; he had turned his head on his
arm to watch something afar off in the sky: and Beric,
following the direction of his gaze, saw a slender skein of wild
geese thrumming out of the morning emptiness. Almost in
the same moment he heard them, a thread of sound at first,
caught and blown about by the upper air, but strengthening
as the dark skein swept nearer, into a vibrant babble, a yelping,
half musical, half eerie, like a pack of small hounds in full
cry.

'It is spring, and the grey geese fly north again,' Jason said; and then, as the lovely wind-curved skein passed almost overhead, 'That would make a fine fresco; but one would need brushes made of comet's hair to catch the living swiftness of it.'

Beric watched the flying skein out of sight, frowning; then, frowning still, dropped his gaze to his friend once more. He had never heard Jason talk quite like this before, and it worried him—worried him badly.

Jason saw the trouble in his face, and said quietly: 'It is only that I dreamed in the night, nothing more.' It was so seldom that one dreamed under the rowing-benches; one laboured like a beast of burden, and slept like one.

'Was it a good dream?' Beric asked.

'It was a good dream.' Jason's quiet gaze drifted back to the sky. 'I dreamed that I was back among my own people, in the days before ever I thought of Rome. . . . There was a little boat that my brother and I had for our own. We painted her like a mallard, with green and purple on her wing-coverts, and the eyes at her bows little and bright like a mallard's. I was dreaming of her. . . . It was just after the winter rains, and the whole island scarlet with anemones—most of all where the olive trees fell back behind the house. They always grew most thickly there. And Briseis, my mother's old slave, had been baking bread.'

The other rowers were well awake now; measured footsteps came up from below; from the foredeck of the *Alcestis* the trumpet sounded cockcrow, and an instant later the call came back like so many echoes across the water from the *Janiculum* and the transports. The convoy woke to life and a quickening hum of activity. The rowers were fed and watered, seamen were busy among the damaged spars and rigging; little boats came out from the settlement, bobbing over the swell, with officers to speak with the Legate, and vegetables for sale. The Legate himself appeared on the poop, speaking with this man and that, pacing up and down, at first with his military cloak drawn close about him, then, as the day warmed

149

to fitful sunshine, flinging the brilliant folds impatiently back
from his shoulders as though they were something that he felt
to clog his movements and hold him back.

The slaves on the rowing-benches watched him, sullenly and
slantwise. They knew, as they knew most of what went on in
the *Alcestis*, that the Master wished to make up-river to a town
where the more serious storm damage might be set right and
they could take on more reserve rowers; for with five men out
of action they would have too few reserves for safety, and the
Janiculum was in worse case than themselves, while one of the
transports had strained a seam. But the Legate would not
brook the delay. They watched his quick, impatient gestures,
heard his slightly raised voice. When, in the Master's judgement, would the seas have abated sufficiently for the oars to be
used? In a day and a night? Very well, then, let the convoy
put to sea once more on to-morrow morning's tide.

During all the long waiting hours of that day the rowers
sat hunched and listless in their places. The brief purpose
that had come to them yesterday had gone down with the
gale. They leaned forward, their arms on their knees; for
the most part seeing nothing, hearing nothing; while Naso
lolled at ease against the mast, with his coiled lash ready in his
hand.

But at dawn next day their respite ended. They were
roused out and fed, and when the order came to make ready
for sea, they had been ready on their benches a long while,
sitting as they had sat all yesterday, staring listlessly before
them. The Hortator, still gummy-eyed from his long vigil,
was in his place, and Porcus, uncoiling his whiplash, had begun
his prowling to and fro.

' Out oars.'

In sullen, drilled unison, the rowers stooped for the oars
housed along the base of the flying-deck, and ran them out
through the oar-ports. On each oar the rower of the outer
watch bent to slip home the thong loop which held the shaft to
its thole-pins. As Jason stooped to the task, he gave a little
dry cough, and instantly all Beric's fears, which had sunk a

little, flared up again. Jason had eaten his share of the morning food; he had seemed much as usual, after the day's rest, and Beric had contrived to make himself believe that nothing more than exhaustion had ailed his oar-mate. Now he realized that something very much more than exhaustion was amiss with Jason.

Half turning, with his hands on the oar-loom, he shouted to the Overseer: 'Here—put on a reserve here. My mate is done!'

Porcus swung round and came striding down the deck, his whip raised. 'Who gives orders on the rowing-benches?'

'I do!' Beric cried. 'My mate is sick, he cannot row. If you keep him at the oar you'll kill him!' He caught his breath, as though plunged into icy water, as the lash flicked his cheek.

'*You* will give orders in this galley!' said Porcus in that soft slurred voice of his. '*You* will say when the reserves go on! You insolent hound! If we kill him, there are plenty more where he comes from; look to it that we do not kill you!'

Again the lash flicked out, stinging like a hornet; but furious as he was, Beric felt the sting of it less keenly than he did the warning pressure of his mate's hand against his own. He turned under the lash to meet Jason's compelling gaze. Jason shook his head slightly, and the look in his face silenced Beric's fury as the Overseer's whip could not do.

He had seen that look on a man's face once before, when he had gone to stand behind Glaucus at the Colosseum and fan the flies off him. He had seen it on the face of a gladiator, down on the reddened sand, and a few moments later the Mercuries had come with their hooks and dragged his body away.

Whitt came the lash again, in a parting cut, as Porcus prowled on. The anchor was secured, and the Hortator's hammer was poised for its first beat. It came down, *clack*, on to the sounding table. With a sob of utter helplessness, Beric bent to the oar.

Through the hours that followed, his heart bursting within him, he struggled to pull for Jason as well as himself; but there was little enough that he could do in that way. He had thought that once they were clear of the estuary, half the rowers would be stood off as usual, and even if it was the inner watch that was relieved, surely they would let him exchange with Jason. But the Legate was in a hurry, and he soon realized that both watches were to be kept at the oars.

The shores of Gaul slipped away on the steerboard quarter, growing gradually fainter, sinking into the sea. It was hard rowing in the heavy swell which still rolled in long, oily curves to the skyline, and the light wind was too far westerly to serve the galley's sail and ease the burden of her straining rowers. Porcus prowled to and fro, tickling them up as a charioteer overfond of the whip might tickle up his team. The Legate stood aloof and arrogant beside the Master, looking towards Britain. 'Curse him!' Beric thought. 'Curse him in this world and the next! There he stands above us, untouched by our agony! We swing to and fro, to and fro; our hearts burst, and we die at the oars, that he and his pretty tribunes may be an hour sooner at their journey's end; and he does not even notice. May he suffer one day as we suffer now, and may our ghosts be there to see it, and laugh, and warm our burst hearts at the sight!'

About the end of the second hour Jason began to cough again. The cough became a wet choking, and he sank forward across the oar-loom, and did not cough any more.

'Jason!' Beric cried. 'Jason!' But Jason did not answer. There was nothing for him to do but somehow keep the oar swinging with his mate's weight upon it, while feet came striding along the deck, and an instant later the watchful Porcus was standing over them. Beric glared up at him, his teeth bared as he struggled with the burdened oar-loom. 'Look!' he shouted. 'Look, Porcus! Did I not say he was sick?'

'Or shamming!' Porcus laughed, and whirled up his whip arm; and the long lash flickered out with a hiss and a *whitt*, across Jason's gaunt, scarred back. 'Up, dog! I'll teach you to sleep at the oar! I'll——'

Jason jerked convulsively under the blow, half raised himself, and then, with a long, shuddering sigh, fell forward again, and lay still. As the whistling lash came down again, Beric released the oar, and with a furious cry flung up his free arm to ward it off. The abandoned oar-loom kicked back and all but swept the next pair of rowers from their bench. The whip-lash wrapped itself round Beric's wrist, and in the moment's confusion he all but jerked it out of the Overseer's grasp. Then there was a rush of feet and Porcus's Second had come to his aid with a couple of seamen. Dimly, Beric was aware that the Hortator's hammer was no longer sounding through the galley, and the rowers were resting on their oars, craning round to see what was happening. He was thrust aside, and the lash was torn from his grasp and fell again and again on Jason's back. But Jason did not stir; and the blood came slowly, very slowly, scarcely at all.

Cursing, the Overseer stooped over him and pulled him back by one shoulder, then let him fall again. ' So he was not shamming,' he said, and turned to the Hortator, who had come up. ' Have to get one of the reserves up after all, sir: this one is dead.'

The other rowers had broken into a sullen muttering, and the sound rose and quickened, half angry, half excited: but Beric had stopped shouting. He crouched very still against the next bench, looking down with hard eyes at his oar-mate's body.

The Hortator took from the breast of his tunic the heavy key which never left its chain round his neck, and stooping, unlocked Jason's shackles. Then he stepped back, with a quick gesture towards the gunwale. The Overseer and his Second took up the dead rower between them.

Beric never moved, never raised his eyes. He heard the splash as Jason's worn body hit the water. That was all, when a rower died at the oar; a splash, and a fresh rower shackled in his place, and the galley going on. . . .

The reserve had been brought up, and stood ready; a powerful, fox-red man. He was thrust past Beric into the

153

place that had been Jason's, and the Overseer stooped for the leg-iron.

As he did so, Beric sprang upon him.

Beric had fought in deadly earnest before to-day: for his place in the Tribe when he was nine years old, for his freedom under the window of Rhodope's store-room; he had fought often enough with his fellows of the rowing-benches—though that had been a casual business, the snapping and snarling of dogs over a bone. But this time it was different. This time, hurling himself upon Porcus with a black beserk fury that saw in him not only the hated Overseer who had killed his friend, but the proud and heedless Legate on the poop, the men who had turned down their thumbs for a gladiator at the Colosseum, the whole pitiless might of Rome; this time he fought to kill.

Taken completely unawares, Porcus went down beneath him with a surprised grunt. Through the red haze beating behind his eyes, Beric saw the man's brutal face upturned, and he ground his wrist-iron into it—that was an ugly trick learned on the rowing-benches—while with his free hand he went for the strong throat. Heedless of the blows the other drove up at him, heedless of the tumult and the hands that grasped and dragged at him from above, he hung on like a hunting dog, watching, through that beating red haze, the broken and bloody face of his enemy begin to blacken.

They dragged him off the Overseer at last, half stunned by a blow on the head, and flung him aside, and as he crouched gasping and shuddering against the flying-deck in the grip of two seamen, with the red rage turning grey as cold ashes before his eyes, he knew with helpless fury, by the sounds of someone crowing and bubbling for breath and then being violently sick, that he had not killed Porcus after all.

There were clipped, authoritative voices above him, and the Master's studded sandals on a level with his eyes; and then the Hortator was unlocking his shackles as he had unlocked Jason's. They thrust him to his feet, and up on to the flying-deck, and along it to the whipping-post at the break of

the fore-deck, every man on the rowing-benches craning round to watch. He felt them watching, as he was shackled there with his arms above his head; sullenly resentful on his behalf, bound to him by the fierce bond of the galley slave, yet with a certain wolfish expectancy, none the less. How many floggings he had watched so, at first with loathing, and then, as he grew hardened, with that queer shameful excitement that seemed bound up in some way with the knowledge that it might be his turn next, though it was somebody else's now.

But this time it was his turn. Porcus, who would not be serviceable again for many days, had been cleared away, and it was Naso the Second Overseer who stepped up behind Beric carrying the whip; not the long stock-whip of the rowing-benches, but the short, many-tailed scourge, every throng of which was jagged with knots which cut like steel. The Hortator and the Master took up their stand a little to one side, and from the poop the remote figure of the Legate looked on with cold impatience of the delay.

After it was over, they left him shackled there for an object lesson, his head hanging far back between his up-drawn shoulders, so that the first thing he saw when he opened his eyes again was a sheet of blue light, which as his sight cleared became the spring sky. He had not been scourged before, and he was vaguely surprised that his back did not hurt more. It was in fact quite numb: but he was filled with a horrible, sick sense of shock, he had a raging thirst, and everything inside him felt broken. Behind him he could hear the rhythmic dip and thrust of the oars, the gasping breaths of the rowers, and all the familiar sounds of a galley under way: but before his eyes was only that empty flame of blue. Little by little he managed to drag his head forward against the strings of fire that seemed to run from the back of it down between his raw shoulders; and above the break of the fore-deck the galley's gilded prow came into his swimming sight, proud and graceful as the arched neck of a swan. He rested his forehead against the whipping-post, between his up-strained arms and shut his eyes. Presently the life began to return to his numbed back, and with the life, a burning agony that made him writhe. His arms felt as though they were being torn out by the roots, and as the hours crawled by, his thirst became a torment that was almost past enduring.

The sun was gone, and the sky had paled from blue flame to the colour of a fading harebell, when at last his shackles were unfastened and he was allowed to slip down in a huddle to the deck. Someone heaved a bucket of water over him, and that cleared his head a little. He was given a pot of sour wine and water and allowed to drink his fill, which revived him still further, though his throat and tongue were so swollen that at first he could hardly swallow. And the Hortator himself, who kept such matters in his own hands, roughly daubed his back with warm pitch that felt like liquid fire at the time, but seemed to ease the pain somewhat afterwards.

Presently he was marched back to his old place, and thrust down upon the bench, and the irons once more locked on to wrist and ankle. Fumblingly, he put out his hands and found the accustomed hold on the oar-loom, and his body swung without thought into the familiar rhythm. Only the man beside him was strange. And for the first time it struck home to him that Jason, who had rowed beside him only that morning, would not row beside him again. If he shifted his hand along the oar-loom, Jason's hand would not come up to meet it. Never, never again.

Your oar-mate died, and his body was slipped overboard, and a fox-headed stranger was shackled in his place: and you went on rowing.

It seemed that the inner watch had been relieved sometime during the day, after all, and now they were going on again, to relieve the outer: and the foxy man slid down on to the deck, leaving Beric alone at the oar. How often Jason had slipped down like that; how often he had slipped down himself and lain at Jason's feet. And now, never any more. The desolation and the hard, hopeless ache of loss rose in him, swallowing up even his bodily misery. But presently it all began to fade. Everything was fading, falling farther and

157

farther away. Even the rhythm of the oars was going from him. And nothing mattered any more. . . .

A gleam of lantern-light fell into his eyes, and he realized dreamily that people were standing over him. He could understand what they said to each other, though their voices seemed to fall down to him from a great distance, but it was quite beyond him to speak, or even show that he understood: and it did not matter. Nothing mattered.

'Here's the other one as good as gone,' Naso was saying disgustedly.

Someone was freeing him yet again from his shackles; someone whose head was a dark blot between him and the light. 'Odd how they do this sometimes, after a flogging,' said the voice of the Hortator. 'Pff! Out like a candle.'

'Any use keeping him?'

'None in the world. He's got barely a score of breaths in him. Even if he pulled round, it would be weeks—maybe months—before he would be fit to row again.'

'Slip him over, then, sir?'

'Might as well,' said the Hortator briefly. 'Save burying him to-morrow when we reach Dubris. If he drifts ashore, someone else can deal with him.'

Hands dragged Beric up by his arms and legs, and he was aware of a grunt, and a backward scuffling that might have lasted for years, or for a single heartbeat—he neither knew nor cared. He was almost unconscious as they slipped him over the side.

XIV

THE HOUSE ABOVE THE MIST

BUT Beric, as Cunori his foster-father had once said, was
not born to be drowned.

The shock of the water on his parched and aching
body, the fiery sting of it in his weals, acted on him like a cold
douche on the face of a sleeper. He went down and down into
the black depths, and came up again with bursting lungs and
coloured sparks dancing before his eyes, but once more
sharply conscious. Drawing in great gasps of air, he trod
water, and quite deliberately watched the stern braziers of the
convoy go by. If he shouted, he might be picked up: but
then there would be the galleys again. Better the sea than
that. The sea would be kinder than man had been. Ever
since he had first tumbled into the water from the shelving
rocks of the Seal Strand, without thought or fear, much as the
seal calves did, the sea had been his friend, and he felt it as a
friend now, the buoyant lift of it under him like a hand
bearing him up. The third transport passed so close to him
that he felt her wash as she went by; but the moon was behind
a cloud, and nobody saw him, and the transports went on.
The *Janiculum* passed at some little distance, the rhythmic
beat of the oars coming to him faintly along the rise and dip of
the water, and the red glow of her stern brazier grew smaller
and smaller in the distance.

He was alone with the dark, swinging seas.

He had very little idea of being picked up, even less of
making land, but he was not in the least afraid. The pain in
his back was growing less, and sometimes he almost fell
asleep, but the part of himself that had taken charge on the
night that he escaped from the Piso house, had taken charge
again, and knew that if he went to sleep he would drown. It

159

would be much easier to let go, and drown; but the part of him that had taken charge was determined that he should not let go.

For a time he simply drifted, waiting for daylight, but the galley had been closer to the shore than he guessed, closer perhaps than the Hortator had realized when he was slipped overboard, and the tidal stream was carrying him shoreward all the while. So it was that, with the moon still high in the glimmering sky, suddenly, and scarcely daring to believe it, Beric saw land! Land in the distance, glimpsed only for a moment as the swell lifted him, then lost again as he slipped down into the hollow; but as he strained his eyes towards it from the next crest of the swell, there it was again, a low shore-line smudged like a silver shadow along the rim of the seas. He struck out towards it, and after that there was no more peaceful drifting, only a heart-bursting fight for life that had suddenly become real and urgent to him again.

But the sea that had given him up unharmed once did so again, and with the moonlight fading into the dawn, very near to his last gasp, he found his feet in shallow water, and staggered up through the lazy creaming surf on to an oyster-pale shingle beach. Among the drifted sea-wrack on the tide-line he collapsed with hanging head. There he was very sick, crawled a little farther up on the beach, and was sick again.

Presently he gathered himself together, and on hands and knees dragged himself on again. He came to a breast-high wall of chalk lumps piled between hurdles, and got over it somehow: he crawled over the broad top of the shingle embankment he found beyond, and rolled down on the landward side, and there, with the hairy grasses under him, and the sea sounding softly behind the wall, he lay where he fell, and sank into a kindly blackness.

It was full daylight when he awoke, but he could not judge the time of day in a world that had no sun and no shadow, only mist. Soft, drifting swathes of mist into which the marsh blurred away and lost itself on all sides, and out of which came

the crying and calling of shore-birds. Beric thrust up on to
an elbow, catching his breath as the pain tore at his back, and
gazed about him in bewilderment. How had he come to be
in this place? His sudden movement startled a heron standing reflectively one-legged on the edge of a shallow pool close
by, and instantly the other leg came down, the great wings
opened, and the bird swept into the air, a crested arrow-head
of grace and power. Beric watched it disappear into the mist.
It was beautiful; it would have made Jason glad, as the wild
geese had made him glad, he thought.

Jason! As though the name had been a key, something
seemed to fly open in his head, and the memory of all that had
happened came flooding through.

He staggered to his feet, the marsh tilting and swimming
crazily around him, and began to run. He stumbled and fell,
and got up again; he floundered into shallow water and out
once more, and still ran on. Behind him was the sea, and the
sea meant the galleys. He stumbled on with bursting heart,
snatching a frantic glance over his shoulder from time to time,
as though he thought to see the *Alcestis* herself, like some nightmare creature as swift by land as by water, come neighing
after him through the sea-smelling mist.

The mist! It was growing thicker all the time. When
first he woke he had been able to see quite a long way, but
now the creeping whiteness had closed in on him, so that his
whole world, moving as he moved, was a few feet of sodden
grass, sometimes a dissolving gleam of water, sometimes the
cry of a bird in the eerie stillness, and always the racing drub
of his own terrified heart. Little by little his panic died, and
he slowed to a stumbling walk, but still the one clear thought
in his mind was to get away from the sea, and he struggled on,
doggedly, in what he vaguely hoped was the right direction.
Then there began to be another thought in his mind, growing
steadily more urgent: the thought of water. There was water
all about him, but it was salt. Somehow that seemed like a
thing that somebody had done on purpose, because they knew
that he was thirsty—so thirsty.

So when, a long while later, he caught faint man-made sounds ahead of him, his first thought was that there might be someone there who would tell him where to find water; or even give it to him; for as he checked to listen, it seemed to him that the sounds were made by men working, and where men worked, there might be water for them to drink. Food too; but he was not interested in food, only in water. He started forward, then hesitated, looking down at himself, realizing for the first time that he was stark naked, seeing himself gaunt as a wolf in a famine winter, his blackened and salt-parched skin, the place on his wrist where the shackle had eaten into his flesh and become a sore. But he must have water. Driven by his desperate need, he started forward again. It seemed to him that he stumbled on a long way without the sounds drawing any nearer; and then suddenly the mist swayed back like a curtain, and they burst upon him terrifyingly close. Right before him there loomed, out of the wreathing whiteness, a small shaggy pony standing stocky and dejected under the great panniers on his back, from which two men were unloading lumps of chalk; but Beric's startled gaze went past them to the mist-silvered outlines of other men beyond, who seemed to be packing the lumps of chalk between hurdles and rough masses of blackthorn, to make a wall like the one that he had come over at dawn.

For a stunned moment he simply stood and stared at the little mist-enfolded scene before him, then, as the pony moved on, and another took its place, he dropped flat and froze. There was no mistaking those leather-clad men on the wall, there was certainly no mistaking the tall figure with the crested helmet outlined against the further mist, who stood looking on. He had all but blundered into a working party of the Eagles.

'This stuff is too small,' the Centurion said—Beric heard him clearly—and then raised his voice to call to someone farther along the line of the wall. 'Ho, Melas! Tell Anthonius we're building a wall, not making a tessellated pavement.'

The mist closed down again, and with no thought now of

finding water, no thought of anything save escape, Beric
stumbled to his feet and lurched blindly away into the drifting
whiteness, with the terror of the galleys once more baying at
his heels.

After that, the mist began to gather inside his head. He
fell more and more often as time went by; but always the fear
of the galleys got him up again, and kept him lurching and
staggering on. He was on sodden salting now; land that
would be submerged at high tide. Perhaps he was going to
be drowned after all; but he was not afraid of being drowned,
only of the galleys. The light was beginning to fade, the mist
to turn cobweb grey. Very soon now, he knew, he must lie
down, and not get up again. And then all at once it seemed
to him that the mist that drifted into his face had a new smell,
a warmer, rootier smell, leaf-mould in it, even a whisper of
woodsmoke. It was a smell that promised shelter, and the
familiar things of forest country, and Beric stumbled towards it
as a lost traveller suddenly recognizing the road home.

The ground began to rise, and almost at once furze-bushes
came looming out of the cobweb mist to meet him; and at
once he seemed to be in another world, with the marsh and
the sea and the galleys shut out. A little farther, he was on
the edge of a small dark pool. He had found so many pools,
but surely this one among the furze must be fresh water. In
frantic haste he dropped beside it, and scooped up water in
his palms and tasted it. It was fresh and sweet: and with a
sob, he dropped his head and began to lap like a dog.

When he had drunk his fill, he stayed by the pool for a
little while. Here, among the dark, sheltering furze, it would
be good to go on lying, and not try to get up, any more. But
even here, with the horror of the galleys shut out, something
dragged him to his feet one last time, and sent him staggering
on. The ground was still rising gently, and all at once the
scent of moss and leaf-mould was all about him, and he was
among the trees: low-growing, wind-shaped oak and thorn
trees, that he felt rather than saw, in the mist and the deepening dusk. Sick and shuddering, crashing through the under-

growth like a wounded beast, he struggled on up the gentle slope, with no idea where he was going, or why.

Little by little the grey mist that had almost melted into the deepening dusk began to grow out of it again; it began to warm around him, taking on the faint colour at the heart of a pearl shell, and he came out of it almost as abruptly as a swimmer breaking surface, into the last soft after-flush of a lantern-yellow sunset.

The gentle lift of the land was levelling out; ahead of him the thorn trees ran on, squat and hardy and storm-shaped; but to the left was open turf, and there, standing out from the thorns as though feeling no need of shelter, with the pale wisps of mist curling almost to its terrace steps, with nothing but empty sky beyond, the long, low huddle of a farm-steading rose dark against the fading light.

The place had an air of being wind-shaped, storm-stunted, like the thorn trees among which Beric stood, by the winter gales that had roared across its low roofs; of being deeply and staunchly rooted, as they were, into the stuff of this high fringe of the marsh. There was a light in the house-place window, and it seemed to draw Beric, as though it were a hand reached out to him, as though the house itself had reached out to him friendly-wise, promising the nearness of his own kind. But what had he to do with men? Men had been none so gentle with him that he should feel the need of their nearness now. Nevertheless, he did need it. The knowledge had been growing in him, for a long while past, that he was going to die to-night; and outcast as he was, he was lonely.

If he could crawl closer, and find some corner to lie down, where he would see the light in the window. . . .

That was the last clear thought he had, but through the fog that seemed to swirl up in his head his overwhelming desire to get nearer to the lighted window must have remained with him, for suddenly, without even wondering how he got there, he found himself on the terrace before the house.

The light shone before him in the dusk; a blurred and swimming square of gold with the feathery branches of a tamarisk spraying darkly across one corner. He groped his way towards it. Then his knees gave under him, and he crumpled up and sank quietly forward on to his face. He twisted over a little, stretching out one hand to touch the edge of the soft stain of light that fell across the terrace, and settled his head on his other arm, with a long sigh.

The next thing he knew was the sound of voices, and a dazzle of strong yellow lantern-light splashing on to his face, and starting to his elbow, he saw two men standing over him.

'A runaway slave by the looks of him, sir,' said the man who carried the lantern.

'Aye, poor wretch,' said the other, in a clear-cut and unmistakably Roman voice. 'And he has been on the run over long, it seems.'

Beric dragged himself to his knees, but could rise no further, and crouched there, glaring up at them with terrified appeal. 'Not back to the galleys!' he begged thickly. 'Not—not back to the galleys!'

The second man stooped quickly and caught him as he began to sway. He looked up wildly into a dark, lean face that seemed vaguely familiar, and began to babble thickly and frantically: 'I'll go away—I'll—oh, don't give me up—not to the galleys!' And then, feeling himself being laid back against the man's knee, twisted over with a yelp of pain.

There was an instant's complete silence, and then he felt himself eased gently over on to his face. 'Great God Mithras!' said the Roman voice above him. 'Look at his back!—oh, look at this, Servius; he's been scourged.'

'Happen that is why he's on the run,' said the man with the lantern.

Beric began to babble again: 'Don't send me back. I've never done you any harm! Don't—don't——' Everything seemed slipping away from him, and he fought to hold the world together for yet one moment. 'Not back to the galleys!'

A hand came down on his shoulder, well out beyond the havoc of the scourge, the firm pressure of it seeming for a

moment to steady the world again; and the Roman voice was in his ears, speaking very clearly and insistingly as though to reach him from a long distance and make him understand. ' Listen; there is nothing to be afraid of. You are not going back to the galleys.'

And then the darkness broke over him in a great slow wave.

. . . . .

Beric was chained to his oar again, with Jason rowing beside him, and the seas racing mountains high along the *Alcestis*'s dipping gunwale, and he cried out to the Hortator, ' We must lay the oars in! Some of us will be killed—killed—killed! ' And then it was Jason crying above the storm: ' Life is none so sweet on the rowing-benches,' and beginning to cough; and his coughing going farther and farther away. And Beric was left chained to his bench and calling wildly after him: ' Jason! *Jason!* '

Over and over again it happened. And yet in between whiles he would be dimly aware of some place that was not the *Alcestis*'s rowing-deck, and of people near him who were not his fellow galley-slaves nor yet Porcus the Overseer; and even the taste of warm milk. But always the *Alcestis* would draw him back again; out into dark waters.

' Some of us will be killed—killed—killed! '

' Life is none so sweet on the rowing-benches.'

And then the last time of all, as he struggled against his chains, calling frantically after his lost oar-mate, suddenly Jason was beside him again, saying: ' Look! we thought that they were iron, but all the while they were only made of rushes.' And Beric looked down and saw that his shackles were made of plaited green rushes, and snapped them with a finger. And as he did so, the *Alcestis* changed, dwindling into a little boat like those he had seen on the ornamental lake in the gardens of Lucullus at Rome. A mere cockle-shell, painted with mallard colours, green and purple on her wing-coverts. Then Jason stepped ashore and turned, holding out a hand to Beric, and they went together up a sandy path with the shadows of olive trees lying blue upon it. They walked a

long way up the path, while all the time the pain and terror
and heartbreak fell farther and farther away behind Beric,
until they came to the heart of the island. The shadows of
the olive trees gathered there, and lay like a pool; and a
heron that had been standing one-legged on the edge of the
pool swept into the air, circling upward on swift and powerful
wings; but as he watched, Beric saw that it was not a heron
after all, but a whole skein of wild geese flying overhead.
'There is your fresco,' he said to Jason; and Jason said:
'Did I not tell you they grew thickest here where the olive
trees fall back behind the house?' And, looking down, Beric
saw that all around their feet the ground was scarlet with
anemones growing like points of flame in the silvery grass.
He turned full to his friend, laughing for the gladness that rose
in him. 'It was a good dream,' he said, 'a good dream. . . .'

For an instant he saw Jason's face very clearly by the
crystal light of the dream, with the faint, twisted smile on it,
and then it began to change into another face, as the dream-
light dulled and thickened into tawny lamplight. In a sudden
panic he cried out as he had so often done before: 'Jason!
Jason! '

And a voice said gently: 'It is well with Jason. Lie still
now.'

The face above him was growing clearer every moment:
a dark, hard face with the brand of Mithras between the
brows, out of which eyes that were the cold grey of wintry
northern seas looked down at him with an odd intensity.

Staring up into that dark face, Beric burst out desperately:
'I never turned robber! I only ran away because he said he
would sell me into the salt-mines! You heard him—you were
there——'

'So it *is* you,' said the Maker of Roads and Drainer of
Marshes; and then, as Beric struggled to get to his elbow, bent
and pressed him back: 'Yes, I was there; I heard him. Lie
still now.'

Beric shook his head weakly, gasping for breath. 'I only
chanced on the farm that evening; and Rhodope took me

169

in and—she was kind to me. And then the robbers came, and
the soldiers after them, and the rest got clear, but—I didn't.'

'All this you shall tell me at another time,' Justinius said.
'Not now. Now it is the time for sleep.'

But Beric was beyond the reach of the reassurance in his
tone, knowing only that he was helpless in the power of a
Roman officer; and he thrust out his hands in blind, terrified
entreaty. 'Your soldiers are down yonder—I saw them.
You'll not—you'll not——'

His hands were caught in a hard, quiet grip. 'What is
your name?'

Somehow the very ordinariness of the question reached him
through his fear, steadying him a little. He gulped 'Beric.'

'Then listen, Beric; the soldiers down yonder have nothing
to do with you, nor you with them. Stop being afraid;
there is nothing to be afraid of.' Justinius's voice was deep,
without being either gruff or hearty, a quiet voice, and something in it, and in his hands, began to take effect on Beric,
as the right voice and hands will do on a frightened horse, so
that after a moment he ceased to shudder and his panic
quieted. The flicker of a smile crept into the eyes that held
his so unwaveringly.

'Try to trust me.'

For a moment longer Beric lay rigid, gazing up with
strained, questioning eyes into the face above him; then he
let go his caught breath in a long, shaken sigh, and relaxed.
He trusted Justinius; suddenly he was content to let his life
lie in Justinius's hands.

XV

THE BUILDER OF ROADS AND DRAINER
OF MARSHES

THE next time Beric awoke, it was full daylight, and he found that he was lying on his side with a warm rug over him. The door of the lime-washed cell in which he lay stood open to the outer air, and morning sunlight slanted across the foot of the cot, making the blue and green and crimson chequer of the rug glow with a jewel brilliance. The shadow of a flying bird darted across the sunlight on the floor and he could hear a distant contented clucking of hens. It was wonderful to lie quiet. In a little, moving cautiously, he found that he could even lie on his back, and the discovery pleased him quite absurdly.

Then padding footsteps sounded outside, and the sunlight was blotted out, and there was a woman standing in the door-way. A huge woman clad in a tunic of shrieking saffron, with long swinging pendants of silver filigree in her ears.

In an instant Beric had caught himself together and was crouching against the wall at the back of his cot, wary and menacing as a wild thing cornered, as he glared at her under his brows. 'Who are you?' he demanded hoarsely.

'I am Cordaella. I keep house for the Commander,' said the woman in a soft, throaty voice like a wood-pigeon's.

'Where is the man who drains marshes?'

'The Commander is down with his wall.' The woman came to the side of the cot, billowing all over as she moved, and Beric saw that she carried a bowl and a little brown loaf.

Instantly he was ravenously hungry, but he pressed away from the food distrustfully, his eyes flying back to her face. 'When is he coming back?'

'Maybe this evening, maybe not. He has his quarters

down at the base camp, and once the spring gales are over and the working season starts, often we do not see him for many days together. He will come sometime—between tides.'

'He was here last night,' said Beric defiantly, because he was suddenly afraid that last night had been only part of his dream.

'He has been here every night since he and my man found you,' said the woman soothingly. 'We were afraid, that first night, that you were gone too far to come back. But you came back, and now you are better—so much better. All that you need now is to sleep and to eat, and presently you will be strong again.' She leaned towards him a little, coaxingly, holding out the bowl. 'See, I have brought you some broth —good broth. Drink it before it grows cold.'

Beric still pressed back against the wall, frowning into her face as she bent towards him. It was a kind face, broad and soft-eyed and gentle. Suddenly he yielded, and stretched out his hands for the bowl, with an eager croak.

The broth was good, as she had said, warm and strong and infinitely comforting; and he gulped it down greedily to the last drop, and then, with a long sigh, thrust the bowl back on her, and held out his hand for the loaf.

'Eat it slowly, now,' she said as she gave it to him, 'for it is the first solid food that you have had for a long while past.'

Beric knew that; knew it better than she could do. The loaf was new and sweet, and he sank his teeth into it and tore off about half and swallowed it at a gulp, heedless of her soft protests; then crammed the rest into his mouth as though he were afraid that she might try to take it back again, and demanded, 'Give me more.'

She shook her head, setting the silver ear-rings swinging. 'No more now. You have had enough for the first time. This evening you shall have more, and perhaps an egg. Would you like an egg?'

Beric said sullenly: 'I am hungry now.'

'Aye, poor child, poor child, I do not doubt it. Let you

lie down now, and sleep, and soon it will be evening.' She
set the bowl down on a stool, and began to straighten the rug,
which he had dragged into a tangle. 'Tch, tch. See what a
bird's nest you have made of the blanket. . . . Is it that your
wrist is hurting you?'

'My wrist?' Beric looked down, puzzled, and saw for the
first time that his left wrist was bandaged with strips of linen,
over the place where the shackle-gall had become a sore. The
sight seemed to him so surprising that it drove all thought of
hunger out of his mind. He stared at it wonderingly. 'Did
you do that?'

'No. It is the Commander's work,' Cordaella said, and
repeated her question: 'Is it hurting you?'

He shook his head. 'It burns a little, no more.'

'Then I will leave it alone until this evening. If the
Commander does not come by nightfall, I will salve it again
then.'

'You're kind,' Beric mumbled, looking up at her as one
making a discovery. 'Are you his slave?'

'Neither his nor any man's. I am a free woman, and the
wife of a Roman citizen,' she told him with quiet pride. 'My
man served under the Commander, years ago; and when the
Commander came back to Britain to make grazing land from
the marsh yonder, he took my man back into his service.
Now you have talked enough, and it is time that you slept
again. Do you lie down.'

There was no appeal against her—one might as well appeal
against a mountain—but Beric found that he did not want to
appeal against her. He lay down obediently, and she tucked
the rug round his shoulders as though he had been a small
child; and taking up the bowl, departed with a surging,
billowy motion that was reassuring in itself.

After she was gone, he lay for a little while blinking at
the sunlight across the doorway. His tired mind accepted
quite naturally the fact that he was once again in Britain;
that somehow he had blundered into sanctuary. He un-
tucked the rug again, and put up his left arm for another look

at the bandage on his wrist. The Centurion Justinius had done that. The Centurion Justinius had come up from his wall to do that for him, a galley slave. Some of the lovely quiet of his dream, the quiet at the heart of Jason's island returned to him again, and almost at once he was asleep.

For two days and two nights Beric did nothing but sleep and eat, while the life flowed back into him like wine into a cup. And then on the third day, wearing a tunic of Servius's, he crawled out like an old man into the spring sunlight, and sat on the low step of the terrace. The sun seemed caught in the sheltered angle between the main house-place and the sleeping-wing, and the stones were faintly warm, despite the little wind that stirred the feathery branches of the tamarisk.

But the light which seemed to flow in quiet waves over the lime-washed walls and the low roofs with their powdering of yellow stonecrop was the clear, water-cool light that belongs to marsh country. From where he sat, an open bay of the hillside dropped gently away, forming a sheltered pasture among the low-growing woodland, and at the lower end, where the blossom-bearded thorn trees curved together again, a little red mare was grazing, with her foal beside her. His gaze rested on her for a long time, then slipped out over the thorn trees to the marsh beyond. Somehow he had expected the marsh to be always covered in mist; but to-day it lay clear, spreading away and away, green and grey and tawny, shot through with the silver gleam of water, to the distant shining line of the sea. Away to the right, beyond the farthest fall of the woods, his questing gaze found a grey line snaking out across the sodden flatness, that he knew must be the Wall—the Rhee Wall, they called it. Presently, between tides, the Drainer of Marshes would come up from his Wall again.

Some while later Servius, crossing the terrace with an armful of hay, halted beside him. Both Servius and Cordaella had accepted the coming among them of a fugitive galley slave as something perfectly natural, for whatever Justinius did was right in the eyes of his small badger-grey

174

henchman, while to Cordaella, no sort of stray could ever come amiss. 'Is it the mare, or the Marsh?' asked Servius.

Beric, whose wits had been wandering vaguely along that grey thread of wall, looked up with a start, flinching away an instant as though expecting a blow. 'Both,' he said, recovering himself. 'That is a fine foal she has. Is he part Arab?'

'He is. Antares, the Commander's black, sired him, and *he* is of the strain of the Kailhan, whose descent is unbroken from the stables of Soliman, the King of the Jews. The mare is from the Icenian runs. You'll not find a better cross than that for a chariot pony.' Servius's eyes were crinkled with proud affection as he looked at the small, long-legged creature. He glanced down at Beric. 'You know something of horses, it seems.'

'Yes,' Beric said. 'I know something of horses.'

For a moment he thought Servius was going to ask questions, and he added quickly, with a nod towards the quietly grazing mare: 'Is she the only one?'

'The only one as yet. But there'll be others presently, when we have the long pasture cleared of scrub and back in good heart. This must have been a good farm before it was let run to ruin, and it can be a good farm again. We'll have half a dozen brood mares on our pastures in a few years' time.' Servius shifted the load of hay a little, and took a step towards the edge of the terrace, then checked, glancing back, and asked with a rather gruff friendliness, 'Coming?'

Beric shook his head, and after a moment the other shrugged, and continued on his way.

Beric sat where he was on the terrace steps, watching the stocky, badger-grey figure plodding down the meadow to the low hay-rack: heard him whistle, and saw the mare lift her head and then come delicately towards him. He was lost in a sudden desolation that had come upon him at the other man's words. Until that moment he had looked no farther ahead than the Commander's next coming; now, Servius had let the future in—the future in which the long

175

pasture would be back in good heart, and other mares would graze there with their foals beside them, and there would be no place for him. No belonging place, here, or anywhere. . . . The desolation passed like a sudden chill wind, as swiftly as it had come, but it took with it his sense of sanctuary; and still he did not go down to join Servius and the little red mare.

Justinius did not return that night, nor had he come home the next, when, after the evening meal, Beric went into the long living-room, carrying logs for the fire. Whether or no the master of the house was at home, there was always a low fire burning there, British fashion, on a raised hearth in the centre of the room. It was the Hearth Fire, the living heart of the house. Beric dumped his load, and knelt down beside the hearth to tend it. The flames sprang up as he thrust the half-burned logs together, and the long, bare room warmed out of the shadows; Justinius's big writing-table, his cross-legged camp chair, the carved citron wood scroll-chest by the door, taking shape and substance as the firelight touched them.

Beric sat back on his heels, staring down into the small flames raying marigold-wise from under an apple log. The door of the kitchen-place stood open, and beyond it he could hear Cordaella scouring pots and singing to herself softly and tunelessly the while. Hearth fire and a woman singing to herself while she scoured pots, they were part of a long-forgotten world that he had once belonged to. But that was before the *Alcestis*, long before the *Alcestis*, and he did not belong to that world now.

Cordaella ceased her singing, and he reached for another log, then checked with his hand out, as very faintly he caught the beat of horse-hooves on the track from the camp. Outside on the terrace there would be nothing to hear as yet, he knew, but this long room had a trick of catching sounds. All day long it was murmurous with the voices of the Marsh, as a shell that sings with the sea in it when you hold it to your ear. Many riders might come and go along that track beyond the thorn curve of the wind-break, he knew, for Servius had told him that it linked the base camp with the big road a few miles inland; but somehow he never doubted that it was Justinius. He settled the log on the fire with infinite care, then sprang up, his vague, unhappy sense of being outcast for the moment quite forgotten.

He dipped a twig in the fire, watching as the tip of it blossomed into flame, and then crossed to the tall bronze lamp. The master of the house should not come home to a twilit atrium. He kindled the lamp, and the flame sprang up raggedly, topped with a wisp of switch; the wick needed trimming. He tended it automatically, as he had tended so many lamps in the house of Piso, seeing the flame steady and grow clear, a slim crocus of light, golden petalled and blue at the heart, that sent the distant marsh beyond the open door-way retreating into the twilight.

He was still standing by the lamp when the hooves clattered into the steading yard, and Justinius's deep voice sounded outside, speaking to Servius. Still standing there when steps came along the terrace, and the master of the house appeared in the doorway.

Justinius was in uniform of a somewhat undress kind. He wore no body-armour, only his leather tunic liberally daubed with mud and chalk, and his helmet showed a bare comb without the familiar parade crest. In his fine tunic and banquet-wreath of winter cyclamen at Publius Piso's table, his dark face, long arms, and too great breadth of shoulder had made him seem grotesque; but here, with the twilit Marsh spread behind his squat, bull-shouldered figure, clad in mired leather and bare bronze, he was no longer grotesque, because he was in his own world. He was like the storm-shaped thorn trees of the Marsh fringe, deep rooted and indomitable, and of the same steadfast and stubborn courage.

At sight of Beric he checked on the threshold, a faintly startled look springing into his eyes. Beric had contrived by this time to rid himself of his beard; and Cordaella had clipped off his matted hair, so that now it was short in the

177

Roman fashion. He was clean and fed, and above all, he had been kindly used; and gaunt and haggard though he was, he looked very different from the terrified, wolfish creature who had fallen beneath Justinius's window. For a long moment they looked at each other in silence, Beric standing by the lamp, the Drainer of Marshes stock still in the doorway.

Then Justinius stumped forward, leaving the door open to the spring dusk behind him. 'So. This is famously well. You must be as tough as a mountain pony!' he said approvingly. Then to the enormous saffron-clad figure who had surged into the inner doorway, 'Cordaella, I am come home very late—but at least I need no feeding.'

'I have always cold meat ready dressed for your coming, and there is ewe-milk cheese and a new batch of spice cakes,' Cordaella said tranquilly.

'A banquet indeed: but I had dinner in camp. I need no more than a wash.'

Cordaella heaved a sigh for her rejected spice cakes, but did not protest. 'Servius has taken out the hot water,' she said.

The Drainer of Marshes laughed, already slipping off his heavy cloak. 'You are a wonderful woman, Cordaella. It has long been my belief that you possess the second sight.' He tossed the cloak across the citron-wood chest by the door. 'Wait for me, Beric, I want to look at your wrist when I come back,' and turning he went out again, and Beric heard his heavy footsteps crossing the angle of the terrace to his sleeping-place.

Presently he was back, with his leather tunic changed for one of soft rough wool, and carrying fresh linen and salves, which he set down among the orderly litter on the writing-table. 'I have had to deal with so many sores and gashes and crushed fingers in my time that I am become a reasonably skilled surgeon,' he said. 'Show me your back.'

Beric, who had risen from beside the fire at his coming, drew the bronze pin from the neck of his tunic without a word, and slipped it down from his shoulders. Justinius took and

178

turned him round, and there was a long silence. 'Why was this done?' Justinius asked at last.

Beric said simply: 'I tried to kill the Overseer.'

'Unwise, though possibly justified. . . . I am not going to meddle with these weals; they are healing well enough on their own. . . . Yes—now this wrist of yours.'

Watching the Commander's hands on the bandage, it seemed to Beric more than ever strange and wonderful that Justinius should do this for him, a galley slave; should do it as though he cared. That was the most wonderful thing; not that Justinius should dress his wrist, but that he should do it as though he cared. And presently, when the sore on his wrist had been re-bandaged, still stinging like fire from the cleansing rye spirit, and the Commander pulled his cross-legged camp-chair to the fire and sat down with the sigh of a tired man after a long day's work, Beric squatted down at his feet, content to be with him as his hound might be content.

For a while they sat in silence, Beric staring into the fire, the Commander gazing down at Beric, until a wild-apple log collapsed with a tinselly rustle into the red hollow under it, and as though the small sound had released something that held them silent, Justinius said: 'Beric, tell me what passed between the night of Piso's dinner-party and the night Servius and I found you here under the window.'

Beric continued to stare into the fire in silence for a few moments; then, slowly and fumblingly, for it was two years and more since he had strung more than a score of words together at a time, he began to tell Justinius what he asked. He told about his escape and the farm in the hills, and his trial for robbery, and why it was that he had not told the truth that night. He told about the *Alcestis* of the Rhenus Fleet, and the crossing to Britain with the new Legate, and the gale; and about Jason. About trying to kill the Overseer, and all that had happened after, until he came up through the mist and saw the light in the window.

He had been staring into the fire all the while, but when the story was done he looked up. Justinius was sitting forward with his arms across his knees, gazing down at him. There was a tense stillness about the Drainer of Marshes, and something in his dark face that made Beric catch his breath without knowing why. The words were out almost before he knew it. 'Why is it that you look at me so? That night at Publius Piso's table—and this evening when you came in—and now: as though you sought the answer to a question?'

Justinius smiled. 'I am sorry. You remind me a little of someone I once knew. That is all.' He turned his gaze from Beric as though with a conscious tug, and looked instead into the fire. 'Here is a question for you, at all events: and a large one. Who are you, and where do you come from?'

'I was fostered by the Dumnoni of the far west,' Beric said. 'Before that—I do not know. I think my father was a soldier. He was drowned, and my mother also.'

There was a small, sharp silence, and then, still looking into the fire, Justinius said, 'Tell me about it.'

And that also Beric told, first the story of the long-ago shipwreck on the Killer Rock, and then, with some confused idea that he wanted to give Justinius something and had nothing else to give, the story of all that had come after, right up to Publius Piso's dinner-table. It was a story that still hurt in the telling, which perhaps made it a worthwhile gift, after all.

When he had finished, Justinius remained silent for a time. 'I see,' he said at last. 'Yes, I see. Thank you for telling me, Beric.' Then he got up abruptly, and tramped across to the open doorway, and stood there, his shoulders hunched, staring out into the blue dusk.

And in the silence, Beric was suddenly aware of the sound of the wind, a small, desolate wind that came humming and siffling up from the Marsh, to make a faint sea-hushing in the tamarisk beyond the door.

In a little, Justinius turned again, and came back to his seat beside the fire. He looked suddenly very tired, and he leaned forward, holding his hands to the flames as though they were cold; but his eyes when they met Beric's had lost their strained questioning, and were quiet. It was as though his question, whatever it was, had been answered.

'You have seen Maia and the foal?' he said.

Beric nodded, faintly puzzled by the sudden change of subject. 'He is a fine foal. Like a flame, he will be, when he is grown. It is in my heart that I should like——' he broke off.

'You love horses, don't you?' Justinius said.

'I have lived among them and worked with them, after the way of my foster kind, all my life until—a while back.'

Justinius said, 'Stay and help me break Maia's foal, and the others that there will be, after him.'

.   .   .   .   .

But two evenings later, Beric learned what Justinius's unasked question had been, and it was a bitter lesson in the learning.

He had been working about the steading with Servius all day; and now the evening meal was over, and the day's work for the most part over too; and in the kitchen-place, Servius sat before the hearth, mending a broken bridle, while Cordaella sat down to her spinning, and Beric had come out to fetch more wood for the fire. There was plenty of wood already, stacked in its corner by the hearth, but tired though he was, he couldn't rest. When Justinius had bidden him stay and help break Maia's foal and he had known that he need not go wandering on again into the cold and the unknown, his overwhelming relief had driven out all else; but now, after two days, his sense of unbelonging, of being shut out, was growing upon him again. It had been that that had driven him out this evening from the firelit kitchen-place and Cordaella spinning, into the steading yard in the dusk; and now, standing beside the wood-pile with a lichened apple log in his hand, he wondered rather desperately whether it would always be like this, always the *Alcestis* between him and the world, shutting him out. Maybe when Justinius came up from his Wall again it would be different.

He turned back to the house at last, with as many logs as he could carry. There had been rain earlier in the day, and the ground was soft, so that his footsteps made little sound, and he had almost reached the half-open door of the kitchen-place when Cordaella's voice speaking his name in a soft undertone brought him to a halt. 'Servius, do you—notice anything about Beric?' she was asking, and something in her tone held him where he was, listening.

'I've noticed that he works like a fiend half the time, and the other half stands and stares at the work as though he expected it to do itself,' said Servius.

'Maybe you would find it none so easy to work steadily yourself, if you were used to working with a lash at your back!' Cordaella told him with soft indignation, and then: 'Well enough you know what I mean.'

There was a moment's silence, filled with the low thrumming of Cordaella's spindle, and then Servius said grudgingly, 'Aye, I know what you mean. He's a bit like the Commander's wife, as I remember her. Maybe he comes of the same tribe— the Brigantes are all alike as peas in a pod, to my way of thinking.'

'It is his eyes, and the way he carries his head. . . . Beautiful, she was—and she going against all her kin to wed with the Commander.'

Servius sniffed. 'Women's talk! If there had been aught amiss between her and her kin, would she have taken the cubling back to show them, when 'twas born?'

'Maybe her heart turned to her kin, when she had the cubling to show them.' Cordaella's wood-pigeon voice was soft and troubled with old regrets. 'But I knew there would be no good come of it. There was a robin weeping in the birch tree by the gate as the mule-cart passed out. If the Commander had not been already away up-country to his road-making, I'd have gone to him then and there, to ride after her and bring her back.'

'Think he would have listened to you?' demanded Servius dampingly, and in the tone of one who had heard the story many times before.

' Nay now, that is a thing that we shall never know. Away up-country he was, and before he marched into camp again they were beyond his fetching back.'

' Aye, the fever killed quickly, that summer,' Servius agreed.

There was another silence, and then Cordaella said : ' It is in my heart that if the babe had lived, he would have looked much as this one does, save for the seal the galleys have set on him.'

' Now do not you be getting fancies, my lass,' Servius begged. ' The cubling died with his mother and that was the end of the story.'

' I have begun to wonder, these past few days. 'Twould have been an easy thing for her kin to have told the Commander so, and kept the babe for their own training in the tribe. It is in my heart that the Commander wonders too. What else was it made him look like a man struck by black frost, that first night, when the boy seemed like to die ? ' Cordaella's voice suddenly shook. ' Think, Servius—if it should be ! '

Beric flung the door wide, and strode in upon their startled silence. ' My mother was drowned, and my father was drowned, and it is in my heart that I would I had been drowned too ! ' he said, and crashed the logs that he carried down in their corner. Cordaella gave a soft cry of distress, and half rose from her stool, but he flung past her to the inner door. On the threshold he turned for an instant. ' The Commander is not wondering any more,' he said harshly. ' The Commander knows.' Then he walked straight out through the atrium, and across the angle of the terrace to his sleeping-cell, and pitched down on to his cot.

He lay there for a long time with his head in his arms, thinking, while the dusk flowed up from the Marsh and deepened into the dark. Once, Cordaella's footsteps came to the door, and he knew that she was standing just outside. He heard her sigh, heavy and soft and troubled; and then her footsteps went away again, and he was left to his thinking. He had felt very like a lost dog who has found someone to

N 183

belong to, and it had all been a mistake. It had not been for him at all, the caring in Justinius's hands. He had been a fool to think that it was. What was he, washed up from the galleys, that Justinius should look on him with kindness for his own sake? Lying there in the dark, the slow waves of bitterness washed over him. There was no place for him here, after all; no place for him anywhere in the world of men that had cast him out, and made him a slave and sent him to the galleys. So he would go to the wild, and be done with men. He would go now.

He had half risen from the cot when suddenly it came to him that he could not go without telling Justinius. He was not at all sure why, but he knew that he could not. In the morning he would find Justinius and tell him, and then he would go, and it would all be over.

He lay down again, with the quietness of utter desolation, and went to sleep.

XVI

ANOTHER STRAY

H E woke in the first water-cool light of morning, with
the green plover crying over the Marsh, and without
giving himself time to think, stumbled up from the cot,
and set out to find Justinius.

It was so early that no one was stirring as he made his way
along the terrace, and he crossed the head of the long pasture
and passed out between the thorn trees of the wind-break to
the track beyond, never looking back. It was better not to
look back.

The track led gently downward, and through the budding
branches of oak and hazel and the twisted thorns with their
fleece of blossom he could glimpse the sodden flatness of
saltings and the silver gleam of mud flats left bare by the tide,
and many waters winding down to the estuary. Presently
the track curved left, turned sandy and ran out into gorse and
stunted elder and harsh sea-grasses. And away to the right
was the huddle of a native fishing village, and the slender dug-
out canoes of the fisher-folks drawn up above the tide-line.
But ahead of him the track ran on, curving still, to the gate of
something that he knew must be the camp. Beric halted an
instant at sight of the rough encircling stockade, the square-
set rows of tents and cabins beyond, suddenly afraid to go on
down the track and into this camp of the Eagles, so afraid that
his throat tightened, and he had to swallow and keep on
swallowing. But he must go on if he was to find Justinius, and
after a moment he straightened his shoulders and walked
forward.

At the gate of the camp, under the roughly painted Capri-
corn badge of the Second Legion, a sentry leaned on his pilum
and watched the world go by. Beric stopped before him,

and said a little hoarsely because of the tightness in his throat,
' I want the Commander.'

' Oh you do, do you? ' said the man cheerfully. ' Well,
you'll not get him.'

There was a small silence, and then Beric, his gaze going
past the man into the morning activity of the camp, said, ' If
I come too early, I will wait.'

' You are welcome to, but he's not in the camp. Gone up
to Portus Lemanis yesterday, about the ragstone quarrying.'

' Portus Lemanis? Where is that? '

' Up that way.' The sentry jerked a thumb northward.
' Ten miles and more, round by the weald.'

Beric hesitated. ' When is it that you suppose he will come
back? '

' There now, if he didn't go without telling me! ' said the
sentry, with heavy irony. Then, seeing the trouble in Beric's
face, he changed his tone. ' Is it that it must be the Commander? Centurion Geta would not do? He is down at the
sluice-bank now.'

' No, it is for the Commander. I will come back. It is a
small matter,' Beric said.

As he turned away, he knew that the sentry was staring after
him; and suddenly he felt the betraying weals on his back
burning through his tunic, and it was all he could do not to
run.

He had been a fool to follow Justinius down here, of course;
even if he had found him in camp, the Commander would
have had more important things to think about than the
affairs of such as Beric. But what now? He did not know.
He started back the way he had come, then without any idea
why he did so turned into a faint path that sniped off to the
right. A few paces brought him to a small, still pool among
the furze and elder, and after standing irresolutely on the
brink for a little while, he sat down beside it. It did not seem
to matter very much what he did. He was simply drifting.

It was not until he had been sitting there some time that
he became aware of a mingling of sounds drifting up from the

Marsh below him. For a while he paid no heed to it, then, with a kind of dreary half-interest, shifted to one side, and parting the elder scrub looked down on a scene of ordered activity framed in the budding branches. Less than a sling-throw away, where the higher ground sank at last into the Marsh, he saw the squat grey mass of a ragstone sluice set into the toe of the gentle slope, the inlet channel behind it leading out northward into the enclosed Marsh, the outlet curving south into the saltings towards the estuary. And from the outer side of the sluice itself, a low guard wall formed of a double row of hurdles and thorn faggots ran seaward, dwindling thread-thin into the distance, reinforced after maybe a mile by the start of the main shingle bank, before both were lost in the greater distance beyond. All along the guard wall he saw a constant two-way trickle of pack-ponies, outward bound, their canvas panniers laden with chalk that gleamed rawly white against the soft tawny of the Marsh, or winding home with their panniers hanging empty; while all along the guard-wall men were at work unloading them and packing the rough chalk lumps between the hurdles. Then the figure of a tall Centurion appeared, and the scene was complete; the scene that he had stumbled on in the mist, six days ago—or ten—or twelve; he did not know.

He let the elder-scrub sway together again, and turned back to the pool.

Presently a group of girls came to draw water: tall British girls with bracelets of bronze and silver and bright blue glass on their arms. Some of them looked at Beric, but without any particular curiosity, for they saw many strangers these days. One of them smiled at him; but he did not smile back, for the reek of the *Alcestis* rowing-deck rose between him and them. And the girls went away again. But still Beric sat by the pool, hopeless, and yet with a confused and un-reasoning hope that Justinius might return and set the whole world right.

By and by a little half-starved grey cur came timidly oozing to his feet, just as the mongrel in the slave-market had done, and as he had done then, drawn by the fellowship of outcast for outcast, Beric reached out to fondle her. She whined softly, flattening under his hand, shivering and pressing against him, and at last crawled into the long grass beside him, and went to sleep.

The tide that had been low when he came to the pool flowed in over the saltings, and the men and ponies went back to camp. It spread quietly through the chalk and hurdles of the guard-wall, and all along the landward side of the Marsh. It began to fall again; and then at last Beric got slowly to his feet. What was the use of waiting, after all? It did not really matter what Justinius thought of him; Justinius would be glad to find him gone. Better to go now.

He turned back towards the track.

Lost in his own private wilderness, he made his way up through the furze and wind-stunted elder, so blind and deaf to the world around him that he never heard the light smother of many small hooves on the track, until, thrusting through a dense mass of blackthorn, he blundered out into the very midst of a string of pack-ponies coming down at a trot towards the camp.

What happened then was so quick and confused that it was over almost before he knew what it was all about. There was a warning shout, a flurry of trampling hooves, and the shrill squeal of a startled pony as it went up in a rearing turn and plunged back on the pony behind it. Beric caught a moment's swift impression of up-flung heads and tossed manes, a plunging chaos of men and ponies, as he leapt clear; and in the same instant heard an agonized yelp from the many-legged midst of the tumult. He swung round to see the little cur who had come to him by the pool, flung clear, and struggling to her feet with yelp on yelp of pain and terror.

' Hell and the Furies! What is it that you think you are doing, charging out into the track like that?' someone shouted; but Beric paid no heed: he was on his knees beside the little mongrel.

One of the drivers was struggling with a scared and angry

pony mare almost on top of him. 'Aie—Aie—Aie—softly, softly now! Be still, daughter of the Dark One!' But Beric barely heard him, and a few moments later, as the turmoil began to die down, the tall tribesman in charge of the pack-train wheeled his own pony across the track to him, demanding furiously, 'Are you deaf? Or is it that you wish to have your brains kicked out?'

Beric shook his head impatiently, as at the buzzing of a fly. He was running his hands in sickening anxiety over the little mongrel's body, while she cried like a child at his touch. She did not seem to have suffered any internal hurt, but clearly she had been caught a glancing kick on her left shoulder, for her crying rose to panic when he touched it, and she could not stand on her left foreleg. Maybe it was broken.

'It is one of the strays from the camp. Hanging round, she has been, all winter past,' said the man after a moment. 'She must have been following you.'

Beric was gathering the small object of misery very carefully into his arms. 'She is not a stray,' he said fiercely as he got up. 'She is mine. Mine to me!' And he swung on his heel.

The fretting and unruly ponies, and the swearing men he left behind, simply did not exist for him. The poor little brute in his arms was the only thing that mattered. She was woefully light to carry; her ribs stood out under her staring hide, and all her bones felt sharp and brittle. She had ceased her crying, and lay quiet in his arms, as he carried her up the track and across the head of the long pasture to the steading.

Cordaella looked up from the charcoal stove as he appeared in the kitchen-place doorway, and surged towards him, still carrying a small iron skillet. 'Oh, the gods be thanked that you come back! I have been half out of my wits!—and Servius away since dawn about the new plough or I should have sent him seeking you long since—and what the Commander would say——' She broke off. 'Why, what is it that you have there? A stray from the camp?'

'She is not a stray,' said Beric for the second time. 'She is mine.'

' Since when would that be? ' demanded Cordaella, ruffled out of her usual serenity by the anxious day she had spent.

' Since a while back,' said Beric vaguely. ' She has been kicked on the shoulder by a pack-pony.'

Cordaella looked in silence at the two before her, the haggard young man and the little half-starved mongrel in his arms, and evidently decided that it was no time for asking needless questions, no time for speaking of last night. ' Aiee, the pair of you! ' she said, in her softest and most wood-pigeon tone. ' Is she much hurt, then? '

' I do not know: not yet.'

' Take her into the old byre, and I will bring you some food for her. I cannot have her under my feet in here, or I shall end by treading on her.'

Beric turned back across the steading yard. He had fetched dry fern from the stable and made a nest of it in the corner of the disused byre, and was settling the dog into it, when Cordaella billowed in after them, carrying a bowl.

' Here is milk for her with some bread in it,' she said as she gave it into his hand. ' 'Twill be better than scraps, for her little starved belly.' She stood for a few moments looking down at the two of them with a mountainous tenderness, then turned to the low-set doorway. ' There will be food for you when you come for it. Come soon, for it is in my heart that you will be hungry also,' she told him. Then she was gone.

Beric gave the little mongrel the bread and milk, and when she had licked the last drops out of the bowl, set himself to have another look at her shoulder. The instant his hand came near it she began to cry and shudder as before, but she made no attempt to pull away, nor did she snap, as an injured dog so often does; indeed after a while she put down her ragged head and licked his thumb. There did not seem to be any break, but he could not be sure. He had dealt often enough in the old days with hounds when they were sick or had been fighting, but his hands seemed to have grown dull on the oar-loom, and she was so small—less than half Gelert's size.

Justinius would know, he thought; if only he came home to-night.

Justinius! For an instant he sat completely still, staring straight in front of him. He had brought the dog back instinctively, to the place that had given him sanctuary in his own need, without thought of the fact that he had not been coming back himself. Well, that did not matter now: the only thing that mattered was his fellow stray.

Through what was left of the day, he waited, hoping for Justinius's return. He ate the food that Cordaella gave him and did various jobs for her about the steading, and between whiles returned to the byre to be greeted every time with a piteous whimper and a softly thumping tail.

Evening was slipping into the dark, and the stars were out over the Marsh, when at last he heard the sound of hooves on the trackway. It might not be Antares, but somehow he was sure that it was. Squatting beside his dog, he waited, one hand on her suddenly raised head, as the soft triple beat came nearer. Now the beat changed tone as the horse swung aside from the track. It was Antares; Antares coming across the long pasture, clattering to a halt in the steading yard.

There was a gleam of lantern-light on the beaten earth; Justinius's voice and then Servius's; they must have arrived home at the same time; the wood-pigeon voice of Cordaella, soft and urgent; and then all lost in the clip-clop of Antares' hooves as he was led stableward.

The dog whimpered, her ears pricking under Beric's fingers, and he soothed her, squatting beside her in the thick darkness of the byre. A little time passed, and there was no sound save those that came from Antares' stable.

Beric was in the act of getting up to go in search of Justinius, when tramping footsteps came across the steading yard, a gleam of golden light running before them along the ground, and the Commander himself, with a lantern in his hand, loomed into the byre doorway.

For an instant he checked there, the lantern held high, so that the light of it showered harvest-gold into the farthest corner of the byre. He looked down at Beric, who crouched there, blinking up at him in the sudden radiance; then his gaze dropped lower still, to the little mongrel who had staggered to her feet at his coming, and was pressing back against Beric's knees. Then he tramped in, and set the lantern down on the corner of the old manger. 'Is she badly hurt?' he asked.

Beric still had his hand on her head, as he stared up with strained eyes at Justinius. 'I do not know. She came to me by the pool above the camp, and I forgot about her, but she followed me; and we ran into some pack-ponies on the track. I do not think her shoulder is broken, but I cannot be sure. I—my hands have lost their cunning.'

'Let me look,' said Justinius. He flung back the folds of his heavy cloak and slipped down on to one knee, holding out a hand to the little cur. She pressed away from it, flattening herself against Beric and growling uncertainly.

'Men have not been kind to her,' Beric said.

'She seems to have found one of the breed to rest her trust in.' Justinius was advancing his hand very slowly. 'Poor little lass; nay now, I'll not hurt you.' The growling ceased. His hand was on her neck, moving exploringly down her shoulder and foreleg, while Beric watched, making the discovery, even through his desperate anxiety, that Justinius's hands had the same caring in them now as they had had when they tended his own galled wrist; catching the first glimmering of an idea that perhaps the caring in Justinius's hands three nights ago had not been entirely a mistake, after all. In a little, Justinius looked up. 'No, there are no bones broken; nothing amiss that rest and a measure of kindness will not mend. She has had some food?'

Beric nodded, gulping with relief. 'Cordaella gave me bread and milk for her, when I brought her in, and again a while since.'

'So; that should suffice for the time being.' Justinius rose somewhat stiffly, and stood looking down at them. 'Shall we leave her to sleep, and go back to the house-place now?'

Beric gave his fellow stray a reassuring pat, and rising without a word, picked up the lantern. He knew what was coming, as he followed Justinius out, carefully propping in place the bits of boarding that he had collected to close the lower part of the byre door behind him.

Cordaella had lit the lamp in the atrium, but the ends of the long room were shadowy as always, warming to a mingled glow of lamplight and firelight at the heart. Justinius slipped off his heavy cloak and tossed it across the citron-wood chest, beside his helmet, which already lay there, and tramped across to the fire. When Beric joined him after quenching the lantern and leaving it by the door, he was standing in his favourite position, hands behind back, and bull shoulders a little hunched, staring down into the flames.

There was driftwood on the fire to-night, burning with the blue-and-green flame of salt seas, and mingled with it, the red and saffron of blazing apple-logs that stood for the warm, familiar things of the land. A marsh fire, Beric thought.

Justinius looked up. ' Cordaella has been telling me what happened yesterday,' he said. ' Fool that I was, it never occurred to me that others beside myself might see the likeness.'

' Am I very like her? '

' Sometimes. You seemed very like her when I came home three nights ago, and saw you standing by the lamp. The odd thing is that now I know it for nothing but a chance re-semblance, now also that I know you a little better, it seems to me not so very strong after all.'

Beric said almost defiantly, ' Why should they have kept the cubling from you? '

' For no reason in the world, save, as you probably learned from Cordaella, that they gave me his mother unwillingly in the first place. She was of the Brigantes; a tribe that has never taken kindly to the Eagles. . . . Nay, then, it was a wild notion, I admit; it never touched my mind until the night I saw you among Publius Piso's slaves.' Justinius hesitated, and then went on, almost as though it mattered to

193

him that Beric should understand: 'I went back next morning. There was nothing to be done that night: Glaucus was drunk. I went back in the morning, prepared to get you from him if I had to pull the house apart to do it. But I was too late; you were already gone. I could get no word of you, and I had to sail for Britain two days later.' He broke off, staring down into the flames, and for a moment his dark, hawk-nosed face had an oddly shadowed look, despite the firelight on it. Then he asked in quite a different tone: 'Why did you go down to the camp this morning?'

It seemed like a change of subject, but Beric knew that it was not. 'I went to find you—to tell you that I was going away,' he said steadily. 'But you were not there, and in the end I would have gone without telling you, after all.' He jerked his head in the direction of the byre. 'But for *her*, I should have been well away by now.'

'Then I give her my thanks,' Justinius said. 'Why were you going, Beric? Was it because of what you overheard yesterday?'

Beric nodded.

'Remember, when I bade you stay, it was after I knew the truth about you, not before.'

'I think that you would not turn back from a thing because the living heart was gone out of it,' Beric said wretchedly. 'Beside—it is more than the thing I overheard. When you bade me stay, I was glad, because I had not thought; but now I have thought; I was afraid when I went down to the camp this morning—afraid lest any should know me for what I am. There can be no place within the reach of Rome for a runaway galley slave.'

'For a runaway galley-slave, no,' Justinius said. 'You, however, are in very different case. You were put overboard from your galley for dead. There is no hunt on your trail; the galleys are done with you as surely as you with them. . . . Nevertheless, it is not good to live out one's life, even a little, in hiding. I also have been thinking, and the fruit of my thinking is this: that since you went to the galleys for a

194

crime of which you were guiltless, the sooner we prove it the better.'

Beric caught a sharp breath, and then let it go very carefully. 'Prove it? How—could we prove it?'

'Do you remember Calpurnius Paulus, the ancient Senator who was my neighbour at dinner that night? I have not many friends, but he is one of them. It is in my mind that he is the man to take the matter up.'

Beric stared at him in silence for a long moment, while his whole meaning sank in. 'But—but sir——' he burst out at last, stammering in his desperate urgency. 'Even if he did—if he did, and I were proved guiltless, and the old sentence wiped away—I should be Glaucus's slave again.'

'No, you would never be Glaucus's slave again,' Justinius said. He turned and crossed to his writing-table, and taking a key from the breast of his leather tunic, unlocked a small battered coffer that stood there, and began to turn up the contents. 'When I went back to the Piso house that morning and found you gone, that was the one thing I could do—to make sure that at least you did not fall into Glaucus's hands again. He was naturally most unwilling to sell you to me; but—I know certain things about that young man that he would not wish known to his world.' There was a small, grim smile on Justinius's mouth. 'I am not fond of such weapons, but in the circumstances——' He left the sentence unfinished, and taking a slim papyrus roll from the coffer, tossed it to Beric. 'I had this made out at the same time.'

Beric caught and unrolled it, and remained a long time staring down at the few lines of writing within. It was his manumission, his freedom from the arm-ring. So he had been a free man, when he came to trial in that law-court in Rome, with the mistral blowing. If only he had known!

'The name must of course be altered,' Justinius said. 'I never imagined Hyacinthus to be your own name, but it was the only one I knew you by.'

Beric let the scroll fly back on itself. 'You have carried this thing a long time.'

'I have been near to destroying it, more than once.'
Justinius closed the lid of the coffer, and came back to the fire.
'But I suppose that, against all reason, I hoped that you might
come for it, one day.'

'Oh no, not I, but the son you thought I might be,' Beric
said, hopelessly.

Justinius hesitated. 'I suppose so, yes—in the first place.'

'Better for you that the cubling died. We make poor sons,
we who row the Empire's galleys; living after the ways of
beasts, we forget how to live after the ways of men.' Beric
kicked savagely at a log, and watched the sudden flare of
flame. 'I can find no place here. Let me stay until the dog
is strong again, then let us both go. We shall do better in the
wilds than among men, she and I.'

'Give men a chance, first,' Justinius said.

Beric looked up slowly. 'Why should I?' he demanded;
and all the black bitterness that the years had bred in him
sounded in his voice. 'Men have not given one to me.'

Something flickered far back in the other's eyes. 'I am
giving you a chance now,' he said. 'I am asking you to take
it, Beric.'

'What can it matter to you?'

Justinius did not answer at once; instead, he turned, and
tramped to the door, and stood there, just as he had done three
nights ago, staring out across the darkened Marsh. 'What
indeed,' he said at last. 'Someone accused me once—I
think it was at Piso's dinner-table—of having a marsh for a
wife and a straight paved road for a son; and they spoke
more truly than they guessed. But this is my last marsh,
and next year, when the work is completed, I take my wooden
foil. I have been finding that rather a lonely prospect. . . .
When I came home three nights since, you looked as though
you were glad to see me—not as Servius or Cordaella, but as
someone of my own might be glad. It is twenty years since
that happened to me.' He swung round, looking across the
lamplit room. 'Stay here, Beric.'

Beric stood quite still by the fire, hearing the soft sea-hushing of the wind in the tamarisk as the background to a great quietness. 'I—will stay, Justinius,' he said at last, rather hoarsely.

But the old sense of unbelonging was still with him, even now. He was still a stranger in the world he had once belonged to, shut out by the shackle-gall on his wrist, and all that it stood for. Not even Justinius could change that.

XVII

THE WIND RISES

AT first Beric kept to the farm, but little by little, as the summer passed, he came to spend more and more time on the Marsh, where a great earth-bank was rising behind the guard-wall, closing the last gap in the sea defences. He had a share in raising that bank, working with the British labour team and the pack-ponies in whose panniers much of the earth was brought from cuts along the edge of the Weald. It should have been good to work with free men again; yet by the summer's end Beric was no nearer to being one with them than he had been at first. It was as though the reek of the *Alcestis*'s rowing-deck rose between him and all men, even between him and Justinius, shutting him off from the world he had once belonged to.

But it was not that that had sent him out into the wide emptiness of the Marsh one still September day, instead of spending it at work on the farm, as he usually did when the rest-day came round. It was because he wanted to think, and there was more room for it out there, in the wide, wind-haunted emptiness. He wanted to think about something that had happened yesterday. The mails had just come in, and Justinius had called him into the atrium, and laid a papyrus roll before him, and said: ' We have won, Beric! You can go down and cry it through the camp that you rowed two years in the *Alcestis* of the Rhenus Fleet for a crime you never committed, and that the Senate admits it and wipes it off the tablets. I suggest that you do no such thing, for it is none of the camp's business; but there is nothing under the sun to prevent you.'

The odd thing was that it had not seemed to matter very much. What mattered far more was the thing that had come

after, when Justinius had read the Senator Paulus's letter
aloud to him. It was a long letter, with its legal arguments,
and hard for Beric to understand; but he understood the
important bit.

'The scales were chiefly tipped in his favour by the
extremely fortunate chance that he was seen outside the
house of Valarius Longus, on the night of his escape, by
an old stable slave who knew him. Immediately I set
the needful enquiries on foot, this man, Hippias by name,
came forward to swear that on the night in question he
was crossing the forecourt to a sick horse, when he heard
a sound at the gate, and going to investigate, saw this
Beric of yours through the grill, by the light of the
portico lantern, just as he was turning away. He called
after him, but the boy did not stop. He—Hippias—also
swore to having heard cockcrow from the Praetorian
Barracks immediately after, the wind being in the right
direction. This, of course, makes it well-nigh impossible
that, leaving Rome scarcely by dawn, he should have
been so far north by dusk, when the robbery took place.
When Hippias was asked why he had never spoken of this
before, the Lady Lucilla herself came forward to say that
he had told her next morning, when he brought her a
bundle containing a filed shackle and a silver arm-ring
of her father's household, which he had found under the
gate; and she had bidden him keep silent, lest his telling
should in any way lead to the boy's recapture.'

Beric had listened to the reading of the letter very carefully,
and then looked up and said: ' I was many miles out of Rome
by dawn; and sir—there was no lantern in the portico.'

He was quite sure, thinking it over, that it had been Lucilla
who had thought of the story. Old Hippias was wonderful
with horses, but he had not the kind of imagination that in-
vents lanterns.

Deep in his thinking, he had scarcely noticed where his legs
were carrying him, until he woke to find himself right out on

the seaward fringe of the Marsh. The sun was westering, and with seven miles or so between him and camp, it seemed a good time to be turning home. He glanced down out of habit, to make sure that the familiar little grey figure was at heel, before he remembered that Canog was up at the steading, engrossed in one fat puppy. He would be glad when that puppy was old enough to be left, and Canog could come with him again. He missed the light padding of her paws behind him, and her powers of conversation—she was a very talkative little dog. It was because of her trick of singing—rather as a pot sings when it is near the boil—that he had called her Canog, a little Song.

Perhaps it was because of the silence where the small sounds of Canog should have been, that, as he turned his steps towards Marsh Island, he suddenly noticed how still everything had grown.

Usually there was a constant shimmer of lark-song above the seaward fringes of the Marsh, but no larks were singing now—even the shore birds were silent; even the faint wind-music that seemed always to ring across the emptiness was stilled, a hollow stillness set round with the sounding of the sea beyond the shingle ridge. It was as though the whole Marsh were holding its breath, waiting for something.

Marsh Island was no more than a mile-long lift of land at the southern corner of the Marsh. It rose only a few feet above the surrounding levels, but the great embankment of the Rhee Wall ran out into it, and so did the lesser shingle ridge that came down the shore line from the northern sluice below Portus Lemanis, and beside the low, turf-roofed huddle of fisher huts at the inland end there was a small outpost camp in charge of an optio. It was a half-way fortress at the bend of the Marsh defences, a windswept stronghold set round with shifting sand dunes and falls of wet brown shingle. And this evening, as he came up through the low dunes that fringed its north-eastern end, Beric felt it to be a fortress on the alert, waiting, as the Marsh was waiting.

He was making for the Rhee Wall—it was better to follow

the Wall, after dark, if one was not a Marsh-man born and bred—and usually he would have skirted the island, avoiding camp and village; but to-day, because in a queer way the Lady Lucilla's lantern had warmed something in him, and made him feel nearer to his own kind, he turned a little aside on a sudden impulse, toward the huddle of fisher huts. Then a thing happened that for a while drove all awareness of the strange brooding silence from his mind.

On the edge of the village he came upon a man sitting at the seaward end of the thorn windbreak. The man's face was turned toward the estuary and the sea beyond, and a hound lay at his feet: a huge, brindled hound, whose head went up alertly as Beric drew near, showing the star-shaped blaze on his forehead.

With a sudden odd feeling as though his heart had fallen over itself, Beric checked. The dog had begun to growl—a soft, sing-song warning deep in his throat, that changed suddenly into a shrill whine. And as his master turned a blind face from the sea, he sprang up, crouched an instant, and then flung himself upon Beric, yelping in joyous frenzy.

'Gelert!' Beric cried, and crouched down. He had his arms round the great dog's neck, not for an instant believing that the incredible thing was really happening. It could not be happening; it was a dream! Gelert was thrusting and fawning against his breast, almost beside himself with wild excitement. 'Gelert! Old Gelert!' And Gelert jabbed up his muzzle and licked Beric's face from ear to ear.

But in a little he tore himself free and swerved back to the tall man, who had risen and stood quietly by; then back to Beric in another joyous onslaught: to and fro between them, round and round, yelping and whimpering, his tail lashing their legs. And in the midst of the tumult, Beric was gripping both the tall man's hands in his. 'Rhiada! Rhiada, is it truly yourself?'

'Beric? Is it yourself, then?'

'Oh Rhiada, it is sun and moon to see you! Yes, it is Beric. Feel, then.' He released the other's hands, and stood still, and Rhiada reached out, laughing, and began to run them lightly over his breast and flanks and shoulders.

'Nay, I know by your voice and your hands, and by Gelert's joy. . . . It is yourself and it is myself. But you are a man now, cubling—Aiee! Shoulders like an ox, you have.'

Presently the light, quick laughter, the exclaiming and the breathless half-sentences of their meeting falling quiet, they sat down together under the windbreak, while Gelert, sneezing violently, collapsed panting at the harper's feet.

And Beric drew a deep breath, and understood for the first time that it was not, after all, a dream. 'Rhiada, but what brings you here?' he demanded in utter bewilderment.

Rhiada put up a hand to feel with sensitive fingers for the harp he carried strapped to his shoulder. 'That which brings me anywhere, where there are men to listen to me and my harp. After you—left the Clan it seemed to me that the time was come for me to go also. So I took a boy from one of the villages to be my eyes—Kylan, he is over yonder with the fisher-folk now—and went. I have lived a wandering life since then, playing my harp up and down the land, wherever there are men to listen to me.'

Beric looked round at him quickly. 'Was that because of me?'

Rhiada smiled. 'I had always a mind to see the world.'

'And Gelert? How comes Gelert to be with you?'

'Gelert came to me after your going. He would not run with Cunori's hounds. And so when I left too, I asked him of Cunori. It is in my heart that he knew I should bring him to you, one day; and behold, I have brought him.'

Beric looked down at the great brindled hound, remembering very vividly how he had cried with his arms round Gelert's neck, on the night that the Clan had cast him out. 'Nay, that was long ago, and he lies at another man's feet now,' he said. And Gelert, knowing that he was being talked of, raised his head to look from one to the other, his tail thumping, then dropped his chin back on to the harper's feet.

'Let him choose for himself.'

'He has already chosen,' Beric said, and knew that it was true. After a moment he asked: 'Rhiada, have you ever been back?'

'Twice. I was back at seed-time.'

'How——' Beric began, and checked. He had shut his foster kin away from him so long, they and the old life and the whole Clan that had betrayed him, and now it was very hard to let them in again. Oddly enough, it was because of Lady Lucilla's lantern, which had clearly nothing to do with the matter, that he managed to ask at last: 'How was it with them? With Cunori my foster-father and the sons of his hearth?'

'Well enough,' said Rhiada.

'And Guinear my mother?'

'I heard her laugh, but I think that she has not forgotten.'

'And—Cathlan my Spear-brother?'

'Cathlan has taken a girl of the Clan to wife, and there is a man-child in his hut.'

Silence fell between them, a silence filled with the sounding of the sea, hollow in the unnatural quiet. Then Rhiada asked: 'And you? What brings you to this place?'

Beric did not answer at once; and his eyes went down to the bronze bracelet that he wore to cover the shackle-scar on his wrist. 'I work on the great sea-wall that we are raising to hold back the tides from the Marsh,' he said at last.

'So, all these four years?'

'No, since last spring only. I—was in other places before then.'

Despite himself, his voice had hardened, and Rhiada said after a moment: 'They were not good, those other places?'

'No,' said Beric. 'They were not good.'

Rhiada turned towards him a little, his head lifted, as though he were waiting for something more. Then, as Beric remained silent, he turned back to the sea, saying: 'Tell me about this wall, and this Marsh of yours. Surely it is a fine thing to bring land out of the sea.'

So, sitting with his arms about his updrawn knees, gazing

out over the wandering waters of the estuary, where redshank
and curlew were feeding on the ebb tide, he told Rhiada about
the Marsh. Now that the first astonishment was over, it did
not seem strange to be sitting here talking to Rhiada. Kindling to his theme as he went on, he told him about the huge
banks, and the sluices under the weald, explaining with great
care how the sluice-bank, as it rose, had dammed up the water
behind it, so that now there was a shallow lake along the whole
landward edge of the Marsh, and how the sluices, closed when
the tide rose high, and opened as soon as it began to fall, would
have drained it by next summer. He told him about the
green fringe of pasture along the seaward shore, that was for a
promise of what the whole Marsh would be one day, with the
hungry sea shut out. ' Fine grazing there will be for many
sheep, one day, from the sea-wall to the Weald. That will be
a good thing, to have helped in the making.'

He told Rhiada also, without quite realizing it, a good deal
about Justinius, for Justinius and the Marsh were very much
part of each other. Only he made no mention of how or why
Justinius had taken him as a son into his hearth-place, for that
story was not his to tell; and though Rhiada asked many
questions, he did not ask that. Beric remembered that he
never asked questions that were best not answered; it was one
of the things that made him good to talk to. It was good to
talk to Rhiada now. Somehow telling Rhiada about the
Marsh, about the promise of the Marsh, and the small, windswept steading on the fringe of the weald, made him see it
more clearly himself, and seeing, know suddenly how much it
all meant to him.

A soft puff of wind blew in Beric's face, and he realized
that the waiting quiet was gone, and in its place a faint,
rustling unrest, a sense of coming turmoil. The estuary was
running angry gold, and the sunset burning like a great fire
behind the steep prow of Bull Island, where the Legionaries of
six working seasons ago had made their altar to Mithras the
Bull-slayer, the Lord of Light. Again the wind came up from
the estuary, rustling low through the hairy grasses, and the

roar of the surf at the seaward end of the Island seemed to have grown suddenly louder. Surf on shore and swell in the offing; that meant wild weather somewhere, already. Gelert whimpered uneasily, without lifting his head from the harper's feet, and Beric saw that little shivers were running through him. Gelert knew, and so did the gulls. The gulls had all flown inland.

He drew his legs under him, checked an instant sniffing the air like a hound, then got up. 'It is in my heart that I will be away back to camp.'

'Maybe that is as well, for I think the Marsh grows uneasy.' Rhiada was on his feet almost as he spoke, and set a hand lightly on Beric's shoulder. 'I will come with you through the village.'

As they reached the huddled fisher huts, the sunset was leaping up behind Bull Island like the flare of flame when a log falls on the hearth, and already the village was stirring into action. Along the strand below the huts men were beginning to drag the canoes farther up for safety, the younger women hauling with them, while the older ones gathered in door-holes, murmuring together in hushed tones and staring anxiously into the flaming sky. Somewhere a child cried as though it were frightened. The whole village and the Marsh beyond were uneasy, filled with the beginning of dread.

Rhiada paused, giving a shrill whistle, and instantly a boy of fifteen or so broke away from the men about the canoes and came up to them. He was a tall boy, with a thatch of fiery hair that shone almost scarlet in the wild light, and his eyes were dancing with excitement. 'They say that there is going to be a storm,' he announced to Rhiada, after a long stare at Beric. 'The old headman says that there is going to be such a storm as there has not been on this coast since he was a boy! He says the Marsh knows! What is it you would have me do, Rhiada?'

'Come with me to the edge of the village; I shall need your eyes when I turn back.'

So they went on, with the boy tagging a little jealously behind them.

When they came out from the huts, it seemed to Beric that the whole vast emptiness of the Marsh was full of fire, and awe touched him so that he halted in his tracks. He had seen other wild sunsets on the Marsh, but never one like this, never quite this lurid intensity of colour glowing in the breast-high furze and kindling the tawny levels to furnace gold; the whole world burning under a tiger sky of wind-rippled flame; never this fearful glory that was not so much a sunset as a message—a warning—written in fire across the evening.

'I will come no farther with you,' Rhiada said, checking beside him. 'For you will travel swiftest alone.'

'You will be here—afterwards? You will not go before I see you again?'

'I shall be here,' Rhiada said: and then, 'What is it like, this sunset of which the women whisper?'

Beric was silent an instant. How could one describe this fearful shining, this scorching and piercing radiance to Rhiada in the dark? 'It is fire and wings and a drawn sword,' he said at last.

A few moments later he had taken his leave of Rhiada; Gelert also. Gelert had padded whining after him a few paces, then swung back to his master. And going on alone into the burning emptiness, he knew one pang of utter desolation; and then the thought of small Canog came pattering to comfort him, and he realized that if Gelert had changed, so had he. It had not been the sound of Gelert's paws behind him that he had been missing, as he came up towards Marsh Island.

He passed the outpost camp without meeting anyone, and came down to the end of the Wall. The chalk-stack that stood there ready for use in an emergency glared harshly golden among the flame-tipped furze, but already the fearful brightness was dying, as he struck out along the line of the great embankment. He was lost in a confusion of many thoughts that came and went, eddying and intermingling in his head like the smoke of a windy fire.   The coming storm; the shackle-scar on his wrist; Lucilla and Hippias and their lantern; the green fringe of the Marsh; Rhiada and Gelert.   He had been so sure that the old life was done with; he had shut it out and put up the bars against it, and now . . . Odd how the worst gales seemed to come at seed-time or the fall of the leaf—just when the tides were at their highest.

It was dark when he came to the edge of the drainage strip, and the wind, rising with the dusk, was blowing in long, shuddering gusts from the south-west; and the standing water was ruffled like the feathers of a bird with the wind behind it, mealy pale between the darkness of the Marsh and the darkness of the Weald.   Still tangled in his thoughts, he took to the narrow boarded cat-walk, and so came at last to the sluice under the Weald.   It was low tide outside, and the roar of the water down the outlet channel made a deep undertone to the wind that was moaning up from the dark saltings.   Along the toe of the Weald the furze and elder-scrub were in a turmoil, and the whole night seemed full of fret and shivering and the rising voice of the seven-mile-distant surge.   The camp, when he reached it, was purposeful with drilled activity, as the Legionaries came and went about the usual foul-weather precautions, and in the forum before the Commander's tent men were falling in as though for the march.

The faint gleam of a lantern within the tent threw the long shadow of Centurion Geta on to the canvas by the entrance, and as Beric reached it, he heard the Commander's voice inside.   ' I leave it to your judgement; if conditions become really ugly, you may have to keep the sluice closed.   Better we lose a few days draining, than risk damage to the outlet channel.   Good luck, Centurion.'

' Good luck to you, sir: you'll maybe need it more than we shall.'   The crested shadow slid across the canvas, and Centurion Geta came ducking out under the low flap.

Beric, ducking in an instant later, found Justinius standing by the lantern which hung from the tent-pole, making some adjustment to the chin-strap of his helmet, which he held in his hands. He looked up as Beric entered, and his eyes in the lantern-light had the cool brightness of a man going into battle.

'Ah, Beric! I was hoping you would be back soon.'

'I have been out on Marsh Island.' Beric thrust the wild hair out of his eyes. 'They are saying out there that there is going to be the worst storm that has broken on this coast for years. Did you see the sky at sunset?'

Justinius nodded, his hands still busy with the chin-strap of his helmet. 'I saw the sky at sunset, yes. At least we cannot say that we have had no warning.'

'How will it go with the sluice-bank, sir?'

'I am not afraid for this end of the defences in a south-westerly gale; there is a certain amount of shelter from the Weald and from Bull Island. The danger point is where you have just come from. The Wall is not yet as high as I should like, out there; there is no shelter, and the big seas pitch on to the shingle with nothing to break them.' He had the strap fixed now. He put on his helmet and began to buckle it as he spoke. 'That is why I am leaving Centurion Geta in charge at this end, and taking half the Century out to Marsh Island to-night.'

So that was the meaning of the gathering in the forum and the words that Beric had heard as he came up. 'You feel the danger so great?' he said.

The Commander tested the buckle, and let his hands fall. 'I have a feeling that everything we have worked for is in jeopardy,' he said quietly. 'South-westerly gales there have been before and will be again; this is going to be something more—something that only happens once in a hundred years.' For an instant his eyes seemed to darken in the lantern-light. 'The Marsh knows. The Marsh is afraid.'

Rhiada had said much the same thing, so had the headman out on Marsh Island; but Rhiada and the headman were Celts, seeing as the Celt sees, and from them it had seemed natural. From Justinius, the words, spoken in quiet and deadly earnest, had a rather frightening potency.

He saw the look on Beric's face, and smiled, tightening his belt. 'Blame it on my British grandam,' he said, turning for his cloak.

Beric caught it up and brought it to him. 'I will come out, too, sir.'

'Having but this breath of time got back?' Justinius, busy with the bronze fibula at his shoulder, nodded towards a bowl of loaves and a slab of cheese on the camp table. 'Eat first, then go down to the picket lines. We are turning half the pack-train out, and the ponies will take some handling in this wind. The optio in charge will want every man he can get.'

'What of Antares?'

'Antares stays in camp.' Justinius had already turned to the tent-flap, when his eye fell on a set of tablets lying beside the bread and cheese on the table, and he checked. 'And at this time, of all others, I must needs receive a message from the Commandant at Lemanis, that the new Legate is up there to see off a vexillation of the Legion for service in Germany, and proposes to give himself the pleasure of inspecting my sea defences in two days' time.'

It was a moment before the full import of that piece of news touched home to Beric, and he said: 'The Legate Cornelius Chlorus?'

'The Legate Cornelius Chlorus,' Justinius agreed, his eyes on Beric's face.

The name seemed to fall into a trough of quiet between gust and gust of the rising wind. Beric stood very still, staring at Justinius with wide, hard eyes. Then, afar off, a fresh gust wakened. It came roaring up across the saltings, nearer and nearer, to burst in a booming spray of sound against the canvas walls of the tent. The light of the lantern leapt and swung, sending Justinius's bull-broad shadow licking up the wall; then, as the gust passed on, Beric said levelly: 'It is in my heart that I hope we shall have got our gale over, for him.'

'It is in my heart that I hope we shall have some sea-defence left for his inspection,' said Justinius. 'A sad pity it would be, if he were to get his sandals wet.' Then he was gone, head down into the windy darkness, with his heavy cloak beating like great wings behind him.

After his going, Beric stood for a few moments staring past the glow of the lantern, seeing, not the bare brown canvas of the tent wall, but an aloof, eagle-crested figure on the poop of the *Alcestis*.

He heard an order outside, and the tramp of feet. Then he caught up the loaves and cheese and stowed them down the breast of his tunic, and, quenching the lantern, ducked out himself into the wind and the night, heading down through the camp towards the picket lines.

THE GREAT STORM

DAWN broke over the Marsh, with the gale mounting
steadily, and out at the far end, where there was no
shelter from Bull Island or the Weald, the wind
seemed like a living enemy bent on tearing the little settlement
out by the roots as though it had been a furze bush and whirling
it away into the sea. Beric had been at work with the pack-
train since midnight, loading boulders from the long ridge
behind the sea-wall, which, running north-east as it did, stood
in no danger with the gale in this quarter; and bringing them
across the fringe of Marsh Island, to unload beside the chalk
dump, ready for use if the Rhee Wall started to go. Even in
the shelter of the dunes it was hard to stand, and the small,
sturdy pony that was Beric's charge turned its tail to the
wind, ducking its head and straddling its legs far out, seeming
to be chiefly kept from blowing away itself by the growing load
in its canvas panniers.

Yesterday the warm brown falls of shingle and the grass-
bound dunes had been gay with patches of yellow horned
poppies, with broom and sea lavender and the little almond-
scented convolvulus. They were torn and beaten down now,
broken and whirled away or streaming out flat with the harsh
dune-grasses; and the wind roaring across the dunes drove
before it stinging clouds of sand to blind and choke the men
working there. Beric had never known such a wind; not
even on the wild headlands of his old home; and yet something
in him exalted in it, triumphing wildly and fiercely, because
the Rhee Wall had stood one tide without breaching.

Beric packed the last stone into the pannier on his
side of the pony, and seized its halter. In a sudden lull
of the wind, he shouted to the tribesman who had been

loading on the other side: 'Does this often happen, here-abouts?'

The man—he was old and weather-beaten, with the far-sighted eyes of men used to the sea—shook his head. 'There has not been such a wind as this in my time, nor I doubt there was such a wind in my father's time, nor my father's father's. It is in my heart that there will be women wailing along the coast to-morrow.'

He turned to another pony and driver, that had just come battling up, and Beric urged his own pony round into the wind, and with an arm across its neck, started off yet again on the return trip. Far ahead, he could see another laden pony and its driver, battling into the wind; soon, if he looked back, he would see another behind him. Before long he passed a pony with its empty panniers rolled up and strapped close, heading with its driver in the opposite direction. Then a second and a third. So it had been going on since midnight, while with every trip the wind worsened. Well, this would be the last trip for them; after this would be a rest, and other men and ponies taking over.

Heads down into the wind, Beric and the pony struggled back together along the fringe of Marsh Island, halting at times to lean up against the gusts, plunging forward again when the gusts passed. At last, through the lashing, breast-high furze of the inland slope, they came out below the camp and turned down to the end of the Rhee Wall. Several men were in action around the growing dump; the pony ahead of them was being led away as Beric and his pony staggered up, and the man who had helped with its unloading turned to the new-comers. Between them he and Beric unloaded the weary little brute, and got its wildly flapping panniers rolled close before they carried it clean away. When it was done, the optio in charge jerked his head towards the camp. 'All right. Get him picketed, and turn in.'

In the little outpost camp everything was clewed up and pegged down, secured against the wind and weather. And all at once, as he picketed the pony in the makeshift lines behind the open turf-roofed store-shed, where stakes and hurdles were stacked ready in case of need, Beric found himself remembering the *Alcestis*, her decks cleared for foul weather. The thought of her came to him without any of the old horror. Black beans, and sun-dazzle on heaving water, he remembered, scourge and heart-break—and yet something more; something that the groaning rabble of her rowing-benches had known, the night they fought to save her from the Barrier Sands. A floating hell, the *Alcestis* of the Rhenus Fleet, yes: but he knew suddenly that never a wind would rise in all his life that would not taste salt on his lips and blow back to him, with an odd tugging at his heartstrings, the buoyant lift of the galley, and the straining swing of the white fir oars.

With the pony at last watered and fed, he battled off past the roped stack of thorn-faggots, to the barrack row, which was packed now—as indeed every corner of the camp that offered shelter was packed—with tribesmen and Legionaries off duty and getting what rest they could. Somebody gave him hard bread and a cake of raisins, and he ate them, drank at the communal water-jar, and stretched out thankfully in a vacant corner. Here, sheltered from the gale which howled across the low turf roof, and warmed with the warmth of close-packed bodies, he drowsed among the turmoil, until somebody fell over his legs and he woke to hear, beneath the shrieking overtones of the wind, the long-drawn boom and crash of the seas on the outer slope of the Wall, and knew that another tide was upon them.

The wind seemed higher than ever, and the spray was flying far across the Marsh, as he fought his way out to the picket lines again.

All that was left of that day, all the long night, and all the long day after, the wind screamed across the Marsh; and tide after tide rose, each one higher than the last, and hurled itself upon the Rhee Wall, and sank back only as though to gather strength for the next attack. The foul-weather patrols fought their way to and fro along the Wall, on the outlook for any sign of damage, and somehow men and ponies were fed and watered—water was carefully rationed by now, for the springs on Marsh Island showed signs of giving out, under the extra demand. Time passed like a wild dream. They lost all sense of being part of a world that had other people and other things in it; they were a tiny storm-swept world of their own, with nothing outside their frontier but shrieking grey chaos. Only one thing remained steadfast and constant, and that was the squat figure of the Commander, who seemed, during those wild days and nights, to be everywhere at once; his helmet crammed down on his forehead, his cloak long since abandoned, bringing always a feeling of strength and increase to the men who found him among them.

Night came again, the third night of the gale, and still, as it wore on, the embankment held, though whole stretches of the guard wall had been torn away, and replaced with makeshift hurdle-work by men labouring feverishly between tides. Now the tide was running up again, and in the picket lines Beric crouched with the rest of the British drivers, each man beside his pony, as he had done every time the tide rose toward the Wall. Deafened by long use, he had almost ceased to hear the roar of the gale; there was shelter here behind the store-shed, and looking up past the prick of the pony's ears he could see the bright smear of the moon through the curdled skies that scudded overhead like driven sheep. Sometimes the clouds thinned, and the moon peered through, with a nimbus of murky rainbow colours round it, before they drove across again. Then it began to seem that the skies were standing still, and the moon above them and the dark Marsh below were rushing through the night, on and on—faster and faster——

He realized that somebody was shaking him and yelling in his ear. He did not catch the words, but he had no need to. This was it!

All around him, his fellow drivers were scrambling up. In a daze, he stumbled to his feet, and almost before he was fully awake, was heading down through the furze towards the Wall, with his arm over the neck of a willing but puzzled pony, the

214

P

blown tail of the next a yeasty blur in the dark ahead of him. There were men waiting by the chalk and boulder dumps, to load the pack-beasts; the work went forward with urgent speed in the hurly-burly darkness, and in a very short time, the panniers filled now with glimmering lumps of chalk, Beric and the pony were off again, fighting their way down the Wall.

In the midst of the straggling pack-train laden with chalk and boulders, stakes and thorn faggots, Beric stumbled onward with his arm across his pony's neck, and its wiry mane lashing in his face. He was fighting to keep close in to the foot of the bank, where there was a little shelter from the gale that rushed shrieking overhead, but again and again the gusts sent them staggering out sideways into the Marsh, and it was all that he could do to get the pony's head into the wind again and beat back. He had no idea how far they had to go, knowing only that somewhere in front of them was a breach in the Wall, and it seemed a gruelling long way; but in reality they had not gone far when a faint shout out of the hurly-burly ahead told them that they had reached the place.

The moon rode clear at that moment, and the flying silver light showed them all too plainly the seas breaking clear over the embankment on a front more than a spear-throw wide. And already a ragged hollow was forming in the dark outline of the crest, which grew deeper and broader with every wave that crashed across it and came pouring down to deluge the men below.

The Legionaries were already on the scene, and among the moving shapes, the gleam of moonlight picked out for an instant the squat, purposeful figure of the Commander, striking a spark of fire from the bare comb of his helmet. There were men up in the breach, driving stakes to hold the boulders and great lumps of chalk, while others, well behind the Wall, were filling the big two-man hods with earth. Here also there were men for the unloading, dark shadows starting out of the gale-torn darkness, as Beric halted the pony; hands that tumbled out the glimmering chunks of chalk on to the growing pile by the breach; and then he was round again, urging the pony back the way it had come.

How many times he made the trip he had no idea, but every time he returned with a load he saw that, despite all the efforts of the men struggling to check it, the breach was growing deeper.

He was in the act of turning the pony once more, when the moon rode clear again, and, snatching a glance over his shoulder, he saw Justinius up there in the breach, outlined against the racing sky. Even as he looked, the lip of a green sea swept over the embankment, and for a moment the figures in the breach were lost in a spreading burst of spray. Beric was barely conscious of thrusting the pony's halter upon a shadow that chanced at that instant to be standing near; he only knew that almost before the wind had whipped the last of the spray away, he was up beside Justinius in the crumbling breach.

The gale had ceased to blow in gusts; up here it was one continuous shrieking blast that flattened his breath into his body. The tide, piling in over the saltings, three feet above its normal height at springs, had completely engulfed the make-shift guard wall at the toe of the defences, and was swirling unchecked far up the embankment; the great, swinging seas flinging in blow after blow, as though to pound the Wall to pulp. And Beric, choking with the force of the wind, half blind with spray as he struggled to pack in the raw lumps of chalk, could feel the bank tremble and vibrate under him like a plucked harp-string.

He was happy. He was filled with a wild exhilaration that drove out all the confusion and the dregs of old unhappiness that had haunted him so long. This was a clear-cut and simple fight; a personal fight, for the Wall and the Marsh to which it was a rampart, for the green fringe of pasture along the shore that was a promise of better things. Up here, shoulder to shoulder with Justinius in the breach, he had only one thing to do: to keep out the sea that was doing all in its power to come in.

But for a time it seemed a losing fight. Almost as fast as they piled in the chalk and boulders among the driven stakes, they washed out once more, and time and time again, as they struggled to arm the outer side of the breach with thorn-faggots to break the force of the seas, the waves tore their work contemptuously away. Beric was crouching far out on the face of the bank, driving more stakes in an effort to secure the thorn-work, when a sea greater than any that had gone before came sweeping in.

He saw the upward rush of it coming, white fringed through the dark, and heard a warning yell, but had no time to do more than fall flat. Yet, as it leapt clear of the crest of the Wall, it seemed to hang there, curving over him for an eternity. It was very still in the hollow of the wave, with the tempest shut out; still and thick with the dark pressure of air. He thought, ' Cunori was wrong,' and then something swift and confused and shining, about having at least kept faith with the green fringe of the Marsh. And then the wave curled over.

It seemed to crash down on him with the weight of a world falling. He was blind and stunned and winded. He was being dragged out and down. . . . His hands had found one of his own stakes to cling to; and it held firm. He hung on, feeling as though his arms were being torn from their sockets and his whole body stretched out like a bit of wet leather; and then suddenly the intolerable drag was gone, and he was lying spreadeagled in the breach, wondering vaguely whether he was still alive. Somebody grabbed him, and he scrambled to his knees and began to drag himself clear.

A voice yelled in his ear, something about thinking he was gone that time.

He shook his head, sobbing for breath. ' I was not—born to be—drowned.'

It was almost the last of the great waves, the crown of the tempest; but he had no leisure to notice that, until a long while later he realized suddenly that there had been no big seas over the breach for a while.

The tide was on the ebb!

The tide was going down, and the light was growing, and away over the tossing wastes of water a bar of sodden primrose showed in the east; and Beric realized that the wetness lashing his face was not spray but drenching rain. For this tide, at least, the Wall was safe.

Presently, with the waves barely reaching the toe of the bank, he scrambled down from the breach after Justinius. The Commander was soaked and squelching as the rest of them; daubed from head to foot with chalk and mud; his eyes were red-rimmed in the leaden light of dawn, and there was a jagged tear along his left cheek-bone as though he had come into violent contact with a thorn faggot. He grinned at Beric, his teeth flashing in the blue-black stubble of a three-days beard, and Beric grinned back, suddenly closer to him than he had ever been before, because they had been fighting for the same thing. There were more men around the breach and along the Marsh behind, Beric thought, than there had been before; it must be that a party from the sluice end had come up at some time in the night to swell their numbers. Justinius swung round on them as they crowded about him, making them the thumbs up as he shouted above the wind: ' Brave work, lads: we've done it!' Only those nearest to him could hear the words, but the sign did just as well. They returned it to him, half drowned and utterly spent, but all at once grimly jubilant. For a moment it seemed to Beric that they were triumphing too soon, and then he understood. The wind had gone booming round to the north-west. It would blow itself out before long, and meanwhile there would be no more piling up of the seas against the embankment. The Wall was saved.

Suddenly he was so tired that he could barely crawl. It seemed a very long way up to the camp, and he covered the distance in a kind of daze. But when he had eaten his ration of bread and raisins, he left the others to the short spell of rest that Justinius had decreed, and set off for the village, to see that all was well with Rhiada. The gale was sinking already, but even so, he found it hard and unsteady going, for he was leg-weary; as doddery as a day-old calf.

The furze, as he made his way through it, seemed to have come to little harm; but the thorn trees of the Island wind-breaks, streaming before the dying gale, showed the battle-scars of many torn-off branches, while here and there they had been uprooted altogether. The village when he reached it was a scene of utter desolation, though already there were folk about in the wind and the driving rain, moving among the storm havoc with the fatalistic lack of fuss of those who live by the sea and know what it can do. Huts had been unroofed, and canoes torn away; one lay smashed against the sheep-fold wall. Sand was everywhere, drifted deep between the huts. And looking down across the saltings left bare by the ebbing tide, Beric wondered vaguely why they looked different, until he realized with a queer feeling of unbelief that the nearest arm of the river was not where he had expected it to be, but had cut a new course for itself and now ran close in under the shingle falls of the Island.

A man carrying a spade and a coil of hide-rope checked beside him, his gaze travelling out in the same direction. 'We shall have easier launching for the fishing now—until in another year there comes another storm, and maybe the river goes elsewhere.' He nodded to Beric, and trudged on, leaning into the wind.

Beric found Rhiada sitting beside the rekindled fire in the headman's hut, among women and children, hounds and sheep and poultry; all the village had brought their livestock within doors before the storm reached its height. He was nursing his beloved harp, and Gelert and the boy Kylan and an unknown girl-child all slept against his knees. Beric did not attempt to reach him through the crowded, reeking, smoke-filled place, but crouching in the low doorway where the sand had drifted, he called ' Rhiada.'

Rhiada lifted his head, careful not to wake the three who slept against his knees, and answered softly, ' Beric.'

' Is it well with you? '

'It is well with me. How is it with you?'

'We have saved the Wall,' Beric croaked; and ducked out again into the dying gale. All was well with Rhiada, and they had saved the Wall, and there was nothing more that needed to be said at the moment. Somehow he dragged himself back to the breach, where men were already at work repairing the guard wall, while others laboured on the damaged embankment itself, and Justinius tramped up and down, ankle-deep in churned mud and standing water, directing operations.

The leaden weight of his weariness lifted after a time, and all that day he worked steadily, while the gale died down, and the drenching rain-swathes swept along the Wall, blotting out the Marsh as with a grey, draggle-tailed curtain. The afternoon tide came flooding in over the saltings, driving the men on the guard-wall back on to the bank itself: short, steep seas with wind and tide setting against each other. But the wind that had been an enemy these many tides past was become an ally now, tending, if anything, to hold back the water, so that when it ebbed again, there was little new damage to be dealt with. And every tide after this would be less high than the tide before.

By that time the gale had sunk to a fitful wind that swooped in scattered gusts about the Marsh, driving the rain-squalls now this way, now that, and everything was sodden and spent and oddly at peace. Beric had returned to his pack-ponies, fetching down more big stones from beyond Marsh Island, when, as he neared the Wall again, he saw several horses standing to one side, in charge of a couple of Legionaries, and a little group of officers standing before the place where the breach had been.

There was a big stooping man, whom he had seen before and knew to be the Commandant from Portus Lemanis; a couple of young staff officers wrapped close in their scarlet cloaks, and Justinius, standing as usual with his hands behind his back, looking more than ever squat and storm-shaped by contrast with the man who stood beside him, tall and aloof in the gilded bronze of a Legate.

Beric had completely forgotten, in the press of more important things, that the Legate was coming to inspect the sea defences. He must have come down to the sluice, found only Centurion Geta and his small party there, and hearing what had happened out at the far end, come on to see for himself. With the tide high, that must have meant getting the horses along the cat walk or wading them through the drainage strip; but it would take more than that, Beric thought, to keep Cornelius Chlorus the Legate from carrying out a plan, once made. He checked for an instant, then went doggedly ahead, skirting the ragged hole where the earth had been taken to pack the breach, to the pile close beside the little group, where the loads were being dumped for immediate use.

'And *what* a storm! Zeus! *I* never remember such a wind!' he heard the Commandant's slightly over-ripe voice, as he brought the weary pony to a halt.

'Doubtless you are not alone in that.' The Legate gave the harsh, snapping laugh that Beric remembered well. 'I imagine that we have just experienced one of those storms which become local legend, and are spoken of as " The Great Storm " by the great-grandchildren of the men whose mud huts it blew down. Sea-walls, also, for that matter. Do you know, Commander, I was more than doubtful, when I started from Lemanis this morning, of finding much of these sea defences of yours yet standing.'

'The same doubt occurred to us, at one time,' Justinius said drily.

There was a pause. Beric, unloading on one side of the pony while a sandy-haired tribesman worked on the other, knew that the Legate was watching the men at work on the breach. 'Will you have all safe by the next tide?' he heard.

'Our patchwork has already stood one tide. Before the next rises, the bank will be fully secured.'

'I am no expert, but should the bank not be higher, at so exposed a point?'

'Yes,' said Justinius, with a faint edge to his deep voice.

'It should, and eventually it will be. It would have been by now, if I had ever been allowed more than two-thirds of the men I applied for.'

Beric misjudged his cast, and the stone rattled down the pile again to the pony's feet, making it fling up its head, snorting, and begin to back. He had it checked in an instant, but as he did so, he was suddenly aware that the Legate, his attention caught by the scuffle, had turned from the breach and was watching him. For a moment something seemed to tighten in his stomach; then he looked up, straight into the hard face under the eagle-crested helmet. The face of the man who had killed Jason—he and Porcus and Rome between them. And Beric had tried to kill Porcus because he could not reach Rome or the Legate. But save for Jason himself, it all seemed thin and far off now.

There was no flicker of recognition in the Legate's eyes. 'Hard work,' he said tersely.

'Hard work,' Beric agreed. 'But I've known harder.'

There was something in his tone that the Legate was clearly not used to hearing from native labour when he deigned to speak to it, and his brows lifted a little.

Then Justinius took over. 'Sir, I present to you one of my household, Beric.'

The Legate's gaze was faintly surprised as Beric raised his hand in salute. It moved consideringly over his mired figure and the place where the sodden remains of his tunic had been ripped off one shoulder, lingered on his face, and then flicked to Justinius. 'Your son?'

'Only since the spring,' Justinius said quietly.

'So? You make up for lost time, it seems, by breaking him to your trade the hard way.' The cool gaze flicked back to Beric. 'When you come to drain the Empire's Marshes on your own account, at least none of your men will be able to tell you that you demand of them what you have not done yourself. Do you carry your shield in my Legion? The mud makes a difference, of course, but I think that I have not seen you before.'

224

Beric shook his head. 'I carry no shield in your Legion or any other.'

The Legate's brows rose a shade further. 'Surprising! I should have thought that any son of Justinius, even one dating from the spring——' he left the sentence unfinished, and with a careless, but perfectly friendly nod, turned away to ask Justinius some question about the work. A few moments later the whole party were moving off towards the outpost camp.

Behind them, Beric turned quietly back to the pony. The sodden and desolate levels of the Marsh darkening under a new rain-squall seemed to him suddenly to shine. He felt empty and clean and light. It was like the moment in his dream, when Jason had said: 'See, we thought that they were iron, but all the while they were only made of rushes.' And he had looked down and seen that his shackles were of plaited green rushes, and snapped them with a finger, and gone free. He did not know quite when the thing had happened, nor why; save that the storm and the fight for the Rhee Wall and the green fringe of the Marsh had been in some way to do with it; and the Lady Lucilla and Hippias and their lantern; and Rhiada coming out of the old life with Gelert at his heels and leaving the door open behind him. Those had been the things that mattered. But it was just now, when Cornelius Chlorus the Legate, who did not much matter, had looked at him as one who had never seen him before, that suddenly he had known that he was free. Free of the old unhappy things and the bitterness of betrayal that had been like an evil fog between him and the world. Free of the shackle-gall on his wrist.

'Well, is it a good dream?' demanded the sandy tribesman in exasperation. And he found that he was standing stock still, and staring at the boulder in his hands as though he had never seen such a thing before. It was warmly brown, and the rain had brought up the pattern on it. Speckled like a peewit's egg, it was. Beautiful.

'It was a good dream,' he said, and flung the stone on to the pile.

.   .   .   .   .

In the quiet grey of the next morning, Beric stood with Rhiada and Gelert and the boy Kylan where the track from the base camp ran up into the woods. ' I wish that you would not go,' he said. ' Stay yet one night more, and sing to us again.'

' Nay, I sang to you last night, but it is in my heart that this is no place for songs just now, and I will not eat where I do not sing. I am for the next village up-river, where maybe there will be less of storm damage to come between men and the music of my harp.'

' Rhiada——' Beric said, and hesitated.

' Cubling? '

' Rhiada, you will be going back some time? Back to the Clan? '

' Assuredly, when my wanderings carry me west again.'

' Will you take a message for me, to Guinear my mother? I promised her, on the night they cast me out, that when I had made a new life among my own people I would send her word —once, and not again—that she might know that it was well with me.'

' I will tell her,' Rhiada said. ' Is there anything beside? '

' No. Tell her that I have made a new life among my own people, and that it is well with me, and that I remember my promise. That is all.'

' Maybe it is better so,' the harper said after a moment. He held out his hands. ' Good hunting to you, Beric: the sun and moon shine on your trail.'

' And on yours,' Beric said a little huskily. ' And on yours, Rhiada.' He caught the harper's hands and gripped them, then stooped quickly to rub the great rough head that Gelert was thrusting against him.

A few moments later, Rhiada, with a hand on the boy Kylan's shoulder, had turned aside to follow his own trail; and Beric was striding on alone up the track. Behind him he heard a shrill, protesting whine, but no scurry of paws came after him. Gelert had made his choice.

The storm had wrought less havoc here than out on Marsh

Island, but there were gaps in the woods, and all around him as he climbed the oaks and thorns showed the white wounds of torn-off limbs, while the ground about their feet was thick with leaves and broken twigs and branches. Yet, standing still, with their stripped and tattered arms raised to the tumbled blue and grey and silver of the autumn sky, they seemed to Beric to wear their courage and their triumph as though it were a crown of next spring's green and golden leaves.

The wind-break, too, had suffered. The biggest thorn tree was down, and beside it he found Justinius, who had come up to get a hot bath, surveying the tangled mass of branches. 'We shall have to put in a new sapling,' he said as Beric halted beside him.

Beric nodded, also looking at the gnarled bole and the long, wind-twisted boughs outflung across the turf. 'Has the steading suffered much? What of Maia and the colt?'

'All is well with Maia and the colt, and little amiss with the steading. Like the sluice-bank, we get a certain amount of shelter from Bull Island.' Justinius half turned towards the house, then paused, looking out over the scarred woods to the estuary. 'Winter is on the way. Soon the grey geese will be flighting home from the north; we shall hear them overhead any night now.'

'With the three of us for the work, we shall have the long pasture clear of scrub before the time comes for the spring ploughing,' Beric said contentedly.

Justinius was silent a moment, then, as they turned back together towards the house, he said: 'Beric, how would you feel about carrying your shield in the Legions?'

Beric stopped dead in his tracks, and stared at him with startled eyes. 'Is—that because of what the Legate said yesterday?' he demanded at last.

'In a way, though it had occurred to me before. You meant to join the Eagles once, did you not?'

'Yes.' Beric rubbed the back of one hand across his forehead. 'Yes, I did; but that was long ago, and—there is all that came after. I—I had not thought——'

'It might be worth giving a thought to, now that you are free. There is no need for haste, even for a year or two. There is no fixed entrance age for the Centuriate.'

Moving on again, across the bush-grown turf of the long pasture, towards the warm russet huddle of the steading, Beric was no longer in the least startled; it was as though, after that first blank moment, Justinius's astonishing suggestion had fallen into the place that was waiting for it, and become a familiar part of himself. Half-way across the long pasture, he asked: 'How would it seem to you, Justinius?'

'I should be very content that we work this place together,' Justinius said quietly. 'Equally, I have always hankered for a son following in my old service!'

They walked on in silence.

Whole patches of the lichen-gold tiles had been stripped from the roofs of the steading, and twigs and leaves and small branches were lying everywhere, driven into corners until Servius had leisure from more important repairs to get rid of them. But as they reached the end of the terrace, Beric saw that the tamarisk was still there, the feathery dark branches still dusted with pale blossom; and Canog sat in a brief blur of sunshine against the lime-washed wall, with her fat puppy firmly attached to her.

She raised her head at Beric's nearing, her plumy tail thumping softly, her eyes lustrous in her small, woolly face. She detached herself from the puppy and started to meet him, then swerved back to her son, picked him up by the roll of fat behind his neck, and managing him with some difficulty, for he was already too big for her, came pattering along the terrace and dumped him all a-sprawl on Beric's feet, with the air of one bestowing her treasure on her best-beloved.

And Beric, stooping to pick up the small, fat creature, had a sudden feeling of coming home from a journey. 'This is my belonging-place,' he thought. 'Whether I stay, or whether I go forth again, it will still be here. It will keep faith with me.' And swiftly come and gone as the shadow of a wheeling gull that swept along the terrace, the remembrance of Jason's

Island brushed him by, an island scarlet with anemones after the winter rains.

There came a flicker of saffron yellow in the warm shadows beyond the open house-place door, and Cordaella surged calmly into view, the silver filigree pendants swinging in her ears. 'Your breakfast is ready,' she said, as though if there had been a storm she had not noticed it. 'And I have baked new bread; come you and eat it while it is hot.'